SOCIAL JUSTICE

Grantmaking II

An Update on U.S. Foundation Trends

Edited by
Steven Lawrence
Senior Director of Research
The Foundation Center

CONTRIBUTORS

Tanya E. Coke
Independent Consultant

Scott Nielsen, Ph.D.
Principal
Alexander Nielsen Consulting

Henry A.J. Ramos
Principal
Mauer Kunst Consulting

Sherry Seward
President
Palladium Resources, Inc.

Bradford K. Smith
President
The Foundation Center

CONTRIBUTING STAFF

Christine Innamorato_____ Production Manager
Rachel Lauer_____ Research Associate
Rebecca MacLean_____ Director of Grants Processing
Lawrence T. McGill_____ Senior Vice President for Research
Loren Renz_____ Senior Researcher for Special Projects
Stacy Repetto_____ Research Assistant
Betty Saronson_____ Graphic Design/Production Associate
Daniel Saronson_____ Research Assistant
Jessica Schneider_____ Research Assistant
Bradford K. Smith_____ President
Teri Wade_____ Vice President for Communications

ABOUT THE REPORT

The original research upon which this report is based was conducted by the Foundation Center.
Data from the report may not be cited or reproduced without attribution to *Social Justice Grantmaking II*.
For a complete listing of current research reports produced by the Center, visit foundationcenter.org.

ABOUT THE FOUNDATION CENTER

Established in 1956 and today supported by close to 600 foundations, the Foundation Center is
the nation's leading authority on philanthropy, connecting nonprofits and the grantmakers
supporting them to tools they can use and information they can trust. The Center maintains
the most comprehensive database on U.S. grantmakers and their grants — a robust, accessible
knowledge bank for the sector. It also operates research, education, and training programs designed
to advance knowledge of philanthropy at every level. Thousands of people visit the Center's web site
each day and are served in its five regional library/learning centers and its network of more than
400 funding information centers located in public libraries, community foundations, and
educational institutions in every U.S. state and beyond. For more information, please visit
foundationcenter.org or call (212) 620-4230.

To order additional copies of this report at $40 each, with savings of 20 percent to 35 percent for five or
more copies shipped to the same address, visit foundationcenter.org/marketplace or call (800) 424-9836.

Acknowledgments

This study was prepared by the Foundation Center through the generous support of the Ford Foundation. We gratefully acknowledge the members of the advisory committee who helped to establish the scope of the study, identify critical questions to be addressed in the grants analysis and survey chapters, and comment on the manuscript.

We are grateful to the chapter authors—Tanya Coke, Scott Nielsen, Henry Ramos, and Sherry Seward—who brought tremendous experience and perspective to this updated analysis of U.S. foundation funding for social justice.

This report owes much to the 26 grantmakers and practitioners who participated in the 2008 interviews that provided the basis for Chapter 2 of this report. (See page iv for a list of participants.) Their responses have contributed critical insight into the evolving nature of social justice philanthropy. We are also grateful to the grantmakers and practitioners who provided perspective on the reemergence of human rights in the domestic U.S. context.

Finally, special thanks are due to Christopher Harris, senior program officer at the Ford Foundation, who championed the Foundation Center's updating of the *Social Justice Grantmaking* study, and to the Ford Foundation, which funded this report. Thanks are also extended to INDEPENDENT SECTOR, for the critical role it played in initiating the first social justice benchmarking project. Notwithstanding the contributions of the readers, any misstatement of fact or analysis is the sole responsibility of the authors.

—Steven Lawrence

SOCIAL JUSTICE GRANTMAKING II INTERVIEW PARTICIPANTS

SOCIAL JUSTICE PHILANTHROPY FOR A NEW ERA

American Civil Liberties Union
Bill & Melinda Gates Foundation
Catholic Campaign for Human Development
Center for Community Change
Grantmakers Concerned with Immigrants
  & Refugees (GCIR)
Disability Rights Advocates (DRA)
Ford Foundation
Hill-Snowdon Foundation
Horizons Foundation
Ipas
Jessie Smith Noyes Foundation
Liberty Hill Foundation
Marguerite Casey Foundation

McKay Foundation
Miami Workers Center
Ms. Foundation for Women
National Rural Funders Collaborative
New York Foundation
Open Society Institute
Social Justice Infrastructure Funders/Funders
  Committee for Civic Participation
State Voices
Tides Foundation
USAction
W.K. Kellogg Foundation
Western States Center
Z. Smith Reynolds Foundation

Contents

Acknowledgments _____ iii
   Advisory Committee _____ iii
   Interview Participants _____ iv
Tables and Figures _____ vii
Key Findings _____ xi

INTRODUCTION _____ 1
By Bradford K. Smith

1. BENCHMARKING SOCIAL JUSTICE GRANTMAKING_____ 3
By Steven Lawrence

Documents the process undertaken to create the *Social Justice Grantmaking* studies,
highlights key elements of the new report, and presents the working definition of
social justice philanthropy.

2. SOCIAL JUSTICE PHILANTHROPY FOR A NEW ERA_____ 5
By Scott Nielsen and Henry A.J. Ramos

Identifies critical ideas and questions for grantmakers and advocates at the outset
of a new generation of social justice philanthropy.

3. THE RETURN TO HUMAN RIGHTS _____ 17
By Tanya E. Coke

Explores the factors motivating some social justice organizations and grantmakers
to explicitly bring human rights back into the domestic U.S. context.

4. TRENDS IN SOCIAL JUSTICE GRANTMAKING_____ 27
By Sherry Seward

Examines the dimensions of social justice grantmaking based on a sample of the
largest U.S. foundations and changes in funding priorities.

SPECIAL REPORTS

The Impact of the Economic Crisis on Social Justice Grantmaking _____ 31
The Role of Atlantic Philanthropies _____ 32
Public Policy-related Social Justice Grantmaking_____ 35
Social Justice Grantmaking for Community Organizing _____ 42
Social Justice Grantmaking for Human Rights and Civil Liberties_____ 45
Domestic vs. International Social Justice Grantmaking _____ 49
Social Justice Grantmaking for Rural Populations _____ 73
Social Justice Grantmaking in the Aftermath of the Gulf Coast Hurricanes_____ 76
Public Foundation Social Justice Funders _____ 80

APPENDIX A: Study Methodology _____ 83

APPENDIX B: The Grants Classification System: Tracking Social Justice Grants __ 85

APPENDIX C: Types of Support Classification _____ 89

APPENDIX D: Foundation Center Cooperating Collections _____ 91

Tables and Figures

CHAPTER 4. TRENDS IN SOCIAL JUSTICE GRANTMAKING

Figure 4-1.   Change in Social Justice Giving vs. All Giving, 2002 and 2006 _____ 27

Table 4-1.   Change in Social Justice Giving, 1998 to 2006 _____ 28

Figure 4-2.   Social Justice Giving as a Share of All Giving, 2002 and 2006 _____ 28

Table 4-2.   Social Justice Giving as a Percentage of All Giving, 1998 to 2006 _____ 28

Figure 4-3.   Distribution of Social Justice Funders by Foundation Type, 2002 and 2006 _____ 29

Figure 4-4.   Distribution of Social Justice Funders by Period of Establishment, 2002 and 2006 _ 30

Table 4-3.   25 Largest Social Justice Funders, 2006 _____ 30

Table 4-4.   50 Largest Funders by Share of Giving for Social Justice, 2006 _____ 32

Table 4-5.   Social Justice Grants by Grant Size, 2006 _____ 33

Table 4-6.   25 Largest Social Justice Grants, 2006 _____ 34

Table 4-7.   Social Justice Giving by Major Fields and Subcategories, 2006 _____ 36

Figure 4-5.   Social Justice Giving by Major Fields, 2006 _____ 37

Figure 4-6.   Change in Social Justice Giving by Major Fields, 2002 and 2006 _____ 37

Table 4-8.   Average and Median Social Justice Grant Amount, 2006 _____ 38

Figure 4-7.   Social Justice Giving by Subject and Foundation Type, 2006 _____ 38

Table 4-9.   Change in Social Justice Giving by Major Fields, 2002 to 2006 _____ 39

Figure 4-8.   Comparison of Social Justice Giving by Leading Social Justice Grantmakers, 2006 _ 39

Figure 4-9.   Economic and Community Development, Giving to Subcategories, 2006 _____ 40

Table 4-10.   Top 10 Economic and Community Development Funders, 2006 _____ 40

Figure 4-10.   Human Rights and Civil Liberties, Giving to Subcategories, 2006 _____ 43

Table 4-11.   Top 10 Human Rights and Civil Liberties Funders, 2006 _____ 43

Figure 4-11.   Health Care Access and Affordability, Giving to Subcategories, 2006 _____ 46

Table 4-12.   Top 10 Health Care Access and Affordability Funders, 2006 _____ 46

Figure 4-12.   Educational Reform and Access, Giving to Subcategories, 2006 _____ 50

Table 4-13.   Top 10 Educational Reform and Access Funders, 2006 _____ 50

Table 4-14.   Top 10 Housing and Shelter Funders, 2006 _____ 52

Table 4-15.   Top 10 Human Services Funders, 2006 _____ 54

Table 4-16.   Top 10 International Affairs, Peace, and Conflict Resolution Funders, 2006 _____ 56

Figure 4-13.   Civic Engagement, Giving to Subcategories, 2006 _____ 58

Table 4-17.   Top 10 Civic Engagement Funders, 2006 _____ 58

Figure 4-14.   Crime and Justice, Giving to Subcategories, 2006 _____ 60

Table 4-18.   Top 10 Crime and Justice Funders, 2006 _____ 60

Table 4-19.   Top 10 Environment and Environmental Justice Funders, 2006 _____ 62

Table 4-20.   Top 10 Employment Development and Rights Funders, 2006 _____ 64

Figure 4-15.   Public Affairs, Giving to Subcategories, 2006 _____ 66

Table 4-21.   Top 10 Public Affairs Funders, 2006 _____ 66

Table 4-22.   Top 10 Arts, Culture, and Media Funders, 2006 _____ 68

Table 4-23.   Top 10 Social Science Research Funders, 2006 _____ 70

Figure 4-16.   Change in Social Justice Giving by Population Group, 2002 and 2006 _____ 72

Table 4-24.   Social Justice Giving by Population Group, 2006 _____ 73

Figure 4-17.   Change in Social Justice Giving by Recipient Type, 2002 and 2006 _____ 74

Table 4-25.   Distribution of Social Justice Giving by Recipient Type, 2006 _____ 75

Table 4-26.   Top 50 Recipients of Social Justice Giving, 2006 _____ 76

Figure 4-18. Distribution of Social Justice Giving by Region, 2006 _____ 77

Table 4-27.   Social Justice Giving by Types of Support, 2006 _____ 78

Figure 4-19. Social Justice Giving by Major Types of Support, 2006 _____ 79

Figure 4-20. Change in Social Justice Giving by Major Types of Support, 2002 and 2006 _____ 79

SPECIAL REPORTS

Figure 4-I1. Social Justice vs. Overall Domestic and International Giving, 2006 _____ 49

Figure 4-I2. Domestic vs. International Social Justice Giving by Major Fields, 2006 _____ 49

Table 4-X1.   Selected Public Foundation Social Justice Funders, 2006 _____ 80

Figure 4-X1. Selected Public Foundation Social Justice Funders, Giving by Major Fields, 2006 __ 81

Key Findings

Social Justice Grantmaking II: An Update on U.S. Foundation Trends provides a comprehensive overview of social justice–related funding by the nation's foundation community. It is designed to further both the understanding and practice of social justice philanthropy. The report includes perspective on the opportunities and challenges facing social justice funders, insight on emerging strategies in the field, and detailed quantitative benchmarking of changes in social justice funding, ranging from principal grantmaking priorities to the geographic distribution of funding.

The report updates and builds upon *Social Justice Grantmaking: A Report on Foundation Trends,* issued in 2005. By providing the first-ever quantitative measurement of this type of funding, *Social Justice Grantmaking* moved discussions of the state of social justice philanthropy by U.S. foundations beyond anecdote and laid the groundwork for funders to be able to benchmark this activity going forward. The report also documented the perspectives of leading social justice funders on the state of social justice-related grantmaking during a politically challenging time for social change.

The first *Social Justice Grantmaking* study found that social justice-related support encompassed all areas of foundation activity from civil rights to health to the arts and represented 11 percent of overall foundation giving. At the same time, interviews with 20 social justice philanthropy leaders identified numerous barriers to social justice philanthropy, especially the political climate at the time, the extent of problems relative to available capacity and philanthropic dollars, and a lack of field coherence and new ideas. This had led a number of interviewees to question the terminology and continuing efficacy of social justice philanthropy and a small cadre of these funders to move away from supporting structural transformation and toward a strategic framework emphasizing choice, opportunity, and individual empowerment.

Four years later, the prospects for social justice philanthropy appear markedly improved. While the field accounted for a fairly consistent 12 percent share of overall foundation giving, funders engaged in social justice philanthropy and practitioners working in the field report renewed optimism for the potential of their activities, even as they critically assess their past efforts. They cite a changed political environment, the demonstrated success of a new generation of community organizing in the recent presidential campaign, and new ideas and energy in the field among a number of factors reinvigorating a commitment to social justice philanthropy. Grantmakers and practitioners are also consciously moving away from past practices and strategies that they believe will not effectively serve a social justice agenda going forward.

SOCIAL JUSTICE PHILANTHROPY FOR A NEW ERA

Following years of declining faith in the efficacy of social justice philanthropy, both grantmakers and practitioners are showing renewed optimism. Interviews conducted in 2008 with 18 leading social justice funders and eight advocates/activists provided a set of key recommendations for advancing the field, as summarized below. These recommendations are particularly notable for the frequent overlap between the perspectives of grantmakers and practitioners.

The Funder Perspective

- **Adopt a "Small Tent" Strategy.**

In the past, many multi-issue and multi-constituency collaborations sought to enroll an expansive organizational and stakeholder base—sometimes at funders' insistence. However, these collaborations could be diversity

criminal justice reform

empowerment

environmental justice

human rights

contentious and had difficulty moving quickly. Foundation interviewees identified a burgeoning tendency toward pursuing a strategy of "small tent" collaborations, which contain fewer groups, and are seen to be more nimble and disciplined and provide a higher level of trust and mutual accountability.

◆ **Find Common Ground.**

Many interviewees believe that social justice philanthropy is most effective when it seeks to bridge differences of race, class, language, region, and generation toward a vision of the common ground. Among areas identified by grantmakers as holding promise for bringing together multiple constituencies were health care, economic development, political enfranchisement, education, and environmental concerns.

◆ **Focus on the Grassroots.**

Community organizing continues to be the most prevalent grassroots social justice strategy and warrants much more funding than it receives. Nonetheless, there are concerns among interviewees that many traditional community-based organizations continue to employ a "power analysis" framework that ensures their

stakeholders will remain outsiders. In addition, some place-based foundations have been moving beyond an exclusive reliance on community organizing and are working with a variety of local agents to develop community wealth and other assets of power and influence.

◆ **Do Not Ignore the Political Sphere.**

Although grassroots funding is the priority for social justice philanthropists, some funders note that grassroots support alone rarely yields enough political leverage and expertise to significantly address larger social justice issues. For these grantmakers, providing support for nonpartisan electoral and public sector participation is equally critical.

◆ **Support Identity-based Philanthropies.**

Interviewees agreed that the social justice sector as a whole is underfunded but highlighted identity-based funds as a promising source of new philanthropy. Beyond increasing the resources available for social justice philanthropy, funders believe that these institutions will also change the leadership, discourses, and grantmaking practices of social change advocacy.

Build and Renew the Social Justice Infrastructure.

The importance of supporting an *infrastructure* that sustains and links the work of social justice organizations and grantmakers was referenced by several interviewees. Funders are increasingly supporting ongoing collaboration among national policy groups and their allies working for change at the state and local level. Additionally, multi-issue funders have coordinated with one another, often through funder affinity groups, to support different facets of the social justice infrastructure. Funders appear to be more inclined than in the past to work across strategy or constituency. There is also a growing consensus among funders—and grantee leaders—that the fields of technical assistance and organizational development need to be expanded and updated.

Collaborate with Other Funders.

Grantmakers named greater field cohesion and partnership as the second–greatest social justice priority, behind the need for more core social justice funding. The increased desire for opportunities to network, convene, and collaborate is being sustained in part by new technology that is offering cost-effective ways to undertake peer learning and gain ongoing value from learning communities and other networks.

Collaborate with Grantees.

The move toward closer collaboration is extending to the relationships between social justice funders and their grantees as well. Some interviewees are already making this level of collaboration core to their institutional strategy and operation. However, grantees will also have to be open to change and experimentation. An optimistic sign is that several funders noted a cultural shift as a new generation of nonprofit sector leaders takes over. These younger leaders prefer working together and sharing resources and are, in general, less territorial.

Create Capacity.

All of the social justice funders interviewed for this study agreed that making general support grants to premier groups—multi-year if possible—constitutes the ideal funding strategy. But there was also a rising commitment to capacity building as a way to strengthen organizations, the field, and prospects for sustained social change. The preferred capacity building investment among current funders is leadership development, usually for grantees' executive directors and, occasionally, promising community members.

Plan for a New Generation of Leadership.

Most interviewees noted that the social justice field is at the beginning of a large leadership transition, as baby boomer executives retire. Foundations are increasingly focusing on the development of young leaders to build the bench that will run important nonprofits in years to come. It will be especially important to develop pipelines for the new leaders *within* these organizations. At the same time, senior leaders are often not ready or able to move on. Negotiating this leadership transition and providing ways to continue to engage senior

> *"Funders and advocates are more positive about the prospects for social justice philanthropy to have a meaningful impact than was true just a few years ago."*

Social justice giving grew faster than overall foundation funding between 2002 and 2006

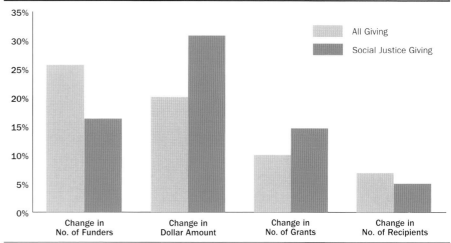

Source: The Foundation Center, *Social Justice Grantmaking II*, 2009. Based on all grants of $10,000 or more awarded by a sample of 1,005 larger foundations for 2002 and 1,263 for 2006.

"[Practitioners] are not opposed to effective evaluation efforts. 'Often the best groups are not encouraged to pursue their best ideas, and weak groups are allowed to limp along. Raise the bar!' "

leaders will be a central piece of social justice organizational development in the next decade.

◆ Re-evaluate the Role of Evaluation.

Some social justice funders find the growing use of evaluations to be counter-productive. A number of funders said that the lack of clear protocols to measure social justice progress and impact creates problems for both funders and their grantees, especially in terms of quantitative analyses. Despite these challenges, most funders believe that evaluation is necessary and useful.

◆ Embrace Mission-related Investing.

Some foundations are using program-related investments and mission-driven investments to augment their grant support for community groups. In the past, these partnerships with business and public sector allies might not have been considered social justice philanthropy at all, since they involve cooperation with sectors often seen as opponents of the priorities of marginalized groups.

◆ Target Underfunded Priorities.

Beyond community organizing, other areas of social justice activity that interviewees considered to be underfunded included

communications and the use of technology, youth and people of color leadership development, mid-career leadership development, convening and collaboration, and technical assistance dedicated specifically to sustaining networks and collaborations. Top-ranked among over-funded organizations according to interviewees were national think tanks and policy groups.

The Practitioner Perspective

◆ Understand the Transformation Taking Place in the Field.

Many of the practitioner leaders interviewed believe that progressives have yet to put forth an updated and broadly compelling vision of the common good. But starting in the early 2000s, social justice advocates changed their strategies in two significant ways that might remedy this gap. First, many more social justice groups became involved in electoral politics. Second, social justice organizations have increasingly focused on communications, messaging, and media relations to build their base and educate the public and decision makers. These changes are moving social change work away from taking adversarial stances to promoting negotiation. Many interviewees also believe that the discipline and sophistication of the Obama campaign as a community organizing event will lead to dramatic changes in the social justice field.

◆ Engage in Strategic Partnerships.

Practitioners feel that closer partnership is possible with grantmakers in ways it has never been before. Increasingly, foundations invite community leaders and organization executives onto their boards and program committees, and program officers help raise money for their leading grantees and find ways to promote sector leaders. At the same time, interviewees feel that the divide between funders and practitioners continues to limit field growth and

Social justice giving accounted for 12 percent of overall foundation support in 2006

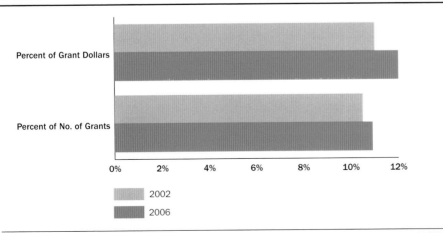

Source: The Foundation Center, *Social Justice Grantmaking II*, 2009. Based on all grants of $10,000 or more awarded by a sample of 1,005 larger foundations for 2002 and 1,263 for 2006.

experimentation, often due to a perception that funders are risk averse. They believe that the key to addressing this disconnect is more opportunities for honest, joint exchange—but not more "show-and-tell" conferences. Most interviewees feel they are a waste of time.

◆ Support Community Organizing and Other Under-funded Activities.

Consistent with the perspective of grantmakers, practitioners too believe that high-quality community organizing is under-funded and undervalued by philanthropy. They also cite civic engagement and election-related activities as being under-funded, especially given recent electoral advances, along with leadership development, litigation, coalition building, investment in rural social justice, and work that builds a global social justice movement. Practitioners think that philanthropy's segmentation in terms of interests and guidelines has contributed to the disconnect between funding and need and call upon grantmakers to think more holistically about the field and work with grantees to establish priorities.

◆ Provide Multi-year, Unrestricted Support.

All of the practitioners interviewed for this study agreed that the way foundation grants are typically made inhibits the field. Single-year project grants are seen as leading to tentative work and inhibiting innovative thinking.

◆ Fund Constructive Evaluation Efforts.

While practitioners may at times feel burdened by current efforts at evaluating their work, they are not opposed to effective evaluation efforts. Several interviewees noted that funders often continue to support weak, less effective groups. They believe that developing evaluation tools that would help to identify which groups are succeeding in their missions and deserve more support is critical.

◆ Connect Think Tanks, Intermediaries, and Small Community-based Organizations.

When asked for their perspective on over-funded social justice activities, practitioners cited similar and sometimes conflicting ideas. Like social justice funders, most social justice groups believe that national think tanks and policy groups receive disproportionately high levels of funding relative to their impact. Intermediaries were also seen as receiving too much support and as being unhelpful and self-interested gatekeepers between national funders and grassroots realities. At the same time, some social justice practitioners believe too many small-issue and -constituency groups are being supported, especially in crowded geographies. Because they are not connected to state, regional, and national allies and may be duplicating the work of other organizations in their area, they tend rarely to be effective in promoting significant social change.

THE RETURN TO HUMAN RIGHTS

For most of the 20th century, social justice advocacy in the United States meant working toward ensuring civil rights. Human rights, by contrast, was generally perceived as referring to the struggles of political dissidents enduring repressive regimes in faraway places. Now a shift in the perceived relevance of human rights to the domestic civil rights and social justice arena is clearly underway. Following is perspective from interviews with grantmakers and practitioners about how social justice and human rights frameworks have evolved and are currently being viewed.

◆ Why the Move to Integrate Human Rights?

Many of the funders and practitioners interviewed indicated that the use of human rights concepts in domestic advocacy is not a substitute for civil rights or social justice, but an

" 'The last 25 years have taught us that we need a more expansive message and course of action. Speaking confrontational truth to power no longer works, if it ever did. Power has no trouble ignoring or punishing us.' "

"Six decades after the creation of the Universal Declaration of Human Rights, there appears to be a return to a more integrated perspective on civil and human rights within the United States."

affirmative enhancement of that vision. They see human rights as a unifying framework that allows for better integration of advocacy strategies (e.g., litigation, grassroots organizing, and policy work) and issue sectors, as well as linkage to global standards and enforcement mechanisms. Grantmakers and practitioners pointed to several useful aspects of the human rights approach including:

· GRASSROOTS LEADERSHIP
Virtually all of those interviewed agreed that the new energy around the application of human rights concepts domestically is being fueled largely by the grassroots. Several organizers noted that the idea that all people are born equal in dignity and rights, regardless of citizenship, race, or economic status, is enormously empowering to vulnerable and marginalized people.

· AFFIRMATIVE, BROAD STANDARDS
Others said that by articulating basic standards of treatment to which all people are entitled, human rights norms provide a set of positive rights that government is obligated to work incrementally to *fulfill*, alongside U.S. constitutional rights *against* discrimination. Some interviewees noted that the emphasis of human rights on equality of outcomes offers strategic benefits in an era in which discrimination is more often structural, rather than overt.

· A FRAMEWORK FOR ADDRESSING ECONOMIC RIGHTS
Leaders in the movement to integrate human rights into the domestic context are small anti-poverty groups that organize around economic justice issues like welfare and housing—concerns that the U.S. Constitution does not recognize as rights. Although the United States has never ratified international treaties recognizing economic rights, some activists nonetheless see these standards as providing useful organizing

principles for their work. Law schools have also begun to explore the application of human rights theories to poverty law practice, training legal services lawyers to deploy international human rights standards along with more traditional claims in welfare-rights and housing litigation. Immigrant worker organizations are also now pointing out that, in a context in which human as well as financial capital flows across borders, international standards are necessary to guard against exploitation of workers in both sending and receiving nations.

· THE PROMISE OF COMMONALITY AND INTERSECTIONALITY
Several interviewees who worked directly with constituents said that human rights encompassed multiple issues relevant to their communities more readily than civil rights, which is often deployed with a single-identity focus. Several grantmakers agreed that the human rights framework is a boon to cross-sector thinking and organizing.

◆ **What Are the Challenges to Adopting a Human Rights Framework?**

Interest in human rights may be rising, but it is still far from the dominant framework for social justice advocacy. Among reasons for the slow adoption of a human rights framework, interviewees cited the fact that human rights treaties still have little traction in domestic courts and legislatures; lingering tensions between civil rights and human rights activists, who for many years seemed content to ignore racial and gender injustices in their own backyard; a concern that the universal frame of human rights will dilute focus on continuing problems of racial and gender injustice; the view that no matter how lacking U.S. human rights protections may be, they far surpass those of many other nations with no rule–of–law mechanisms; and that civil rights or opportunity frames are more consistent with cultural norms.

◆ How Do Foundations View This Trend?

Most foundation interviewees viewed human rights framing as an increasing but still marginal trend. While some grantees have been quietly integrating human rights in their domestic work, many hesitate to emphasize this approach in their grant applications for fear that grantmakers will see it as a naïve or underleveraged strategy. But increasingly, foundations with a history of funding civil rights and social justice are redrafting their guidelines to signal interest in human rights.

TRENDS IN SOCIAL JUSTICE GRANTMAKING

The following analysis examines funding trends between 2002 and 2006 based on all of the grants of $10,000 or more reported by a sample of over 1,005 of the largest U.S. foundations in 2002 and 1,263 in 2006. Grants included in the samples represented approximately half of giving by all U.S. foundations in each year.

◆ Social justice funding grew faster than overall giving between 2002 and 2006.

Providing support for domestic and international social justice activities continues to be an important priority for a number of U.S. foundations. Overall, giving for social justice-related purposes by sampled foundations rose nearly 31 percent between 2002 and 2006, surpassing the roughly 20 percent increase in foundation giving overall. Actual grant dollars totaled $2.3 billion in the latest year, up from roughly $1.8 billion. As a result, social justice-related funding accounted for 12 percent of overall grant dollars in 2006, compared to 11 percent in 2002.

◆ The Bill & Melinda Gates Foundation accounted for over half of the growth in grant dollars.

Numerous factors contributed to the increase in social justice-related grantmaking, from a return to growth in overall foundation giving following the early 2000s economic downturn to the accession of the nation's largest grantmaker—the Bill & Melinda Gates Foundation—into the role of the country's top social justice funder. Between 2002 and 2006, the Gates Foundation's social justice-related giving jumped from $59.1 million to $355.1 million, accounting for well over half of the rise in social justice-related grantmaking. Nonetheless, excluding the Gates Foundation, social justice funding would still have risen more quickly than overall foundation giving during this period.

◆ The top 25 social justice funders provided over two-thirds of grant dollars.

The 25 largest social justice funders in the United States have a significant impact on grantmaking trends in the field. These foundations provided $1.5 billion of the $2.3 billion awarded by all social justice funders in 2006. Together, the three largest funders—the Bill & Melinda Gates

Economic and community development accounted for the largest share of social justice giving by foundations in 2006

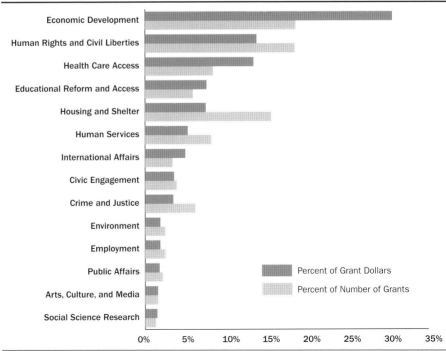

Source: The Foundation Center, *Social Justice Grantmaking II*, 2009. Based on all grants of $10,000 or more awarded by a sample of 749 larger foundations for 2002 and 871 for 2006. Excludes giving by operating foundations.

grassroots health care access
housing rights
economic
development

Foundation, Ford Foundation, and W.K. Kellogg Foundation—provided over one-third of total social justice support. Nonetheless, this tremendous concentration of resources among the largest funders is not unusual. For example, the top 25 international funders in 2006 represented 79 percent of overall international giving.

◆ **Economic and community development topped social justice grantmaking priorities.**

Social justice-related giving spans all areas of foundation activity, but only three areas commanded at least 10

percent of social justice dollars in the 2006 grants sample—economic and community development (30.5 percent), human rights and civil liberties (13.8 percent), and health care access and affordability (13.4 percent). By share of number of grants, economic and community development again ranked first (18.6 percent), but its share was nearly matched by human rights and civil liberties (18.5 percent). The variation in rankings by grant dollars and grants generally reflects differences in the average size of grants awarded in a field. For example, grants for economic and community development, educational reform and access, health care access and affordability, and international affairs, peace, and conflict resolution were far larger on average than in other fields.

◆ **Support rose for all but three social justice fields.**

Foundations increased their support for 11 of the 14 major social justice fields between 2002 and 2006, although rates of growth differed substantially. Two fields doubled in giving: economic and community development (up 109.7 percent) and arts, culture, and the media, including efforts

Nearly 40 percent of foundations' social justice giving funded international activities in 2006

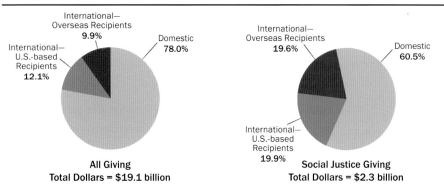

	All Giving Total Dollars = $19.1 billion	Social Justice Giving Total Dollars = $2.3 billion
Domestic	78.0%	60.5%
International—Overseas Recipients	9.9%	19.6%
International—U.S.-based Recipients	12.1%	19.9%

Source: The Foundation Center, *Social Justice Grantmaking II,* 2009. Based on all grants of $10,000 or more awarded by a sample of 1,263 larger foundations.

to increase the participation of underserved and minority populations (up 101.2 percent). Other fields experiencing significant growth included international affairs, peace, and conflict resolution (up 65.4 percent), civic engagement (up 47 percent), crime and justice (up 37.8 percent), and the environment and environmental justice (up 31.5 percent). The three fields experiencing a decline in grant dollars were social science research (down 40.4 percent), public affairs—including support for welfare policy reform and multipurpose policy reform (down 15.7 percent)—and educational reform and access (down 6.2 percent).

◆ **Most social justice grants targeted specific population groups.**

Given the role of social justice funding in addressing social inequities, it comes as no surprise that the vast majority of 2006 social justice grants (84.2 percent) were specifically targeted to benefit one or more population groups. By comparison, less than half (46.9 percent) of grants in the Foundation Center's overall sample were targeted for specific groups. The economically disadvantaged benefited from by far the largest share of social justice support—63.9 percent of grant dollars and 59.5 percent of grants. Ethnic or racial minorities followed with almost one-quarter of grant dollars and close to one-third of the grants. Only two other population groups were targeted with at least 10 percent of social justice grant dollars in the latest sample—children and youth (17.9 percent) and women and girls (11.4 percent).

◆ **Social justice funders were almost twice as likely as funders overall to provide international support.**

A markedly larger share of social justice grant dollars supported international activities in the latest period. Social justice-related funding for U.S.-based international programs and overseas recipients totaled $908 million in 2006, more than double the $440 million recorded for 2002. As a result, internationally focused social justice funding represented 40 percent of grant dollars in 2006, compared to the 22 percent of *overall* foundation grant dollars that provided international support that year. Most of this growth in grant dollars resulted from exceptionally large awards provided by the Bill & Melinda Gates and Rockefeller foundations to introduce the "Green Revolution" to Africa.

THE IMPACT OF THE ECONOMIC CRISIS ON SOCIAL JUSTICE GRANTMAKING

Social justice-related giving by U.S. foundations continued to grow in 2007. Funding for social justice by grantmakers included in the Foundation Center's grants sample reached $3 billion, or 13.7 percent of overall grant dollars that year. (The share of number of grants remained nearly unchanged at 10.7 percent.) Nonetheless, the outlook for social justice grantmaking, and foundation giving overall, changed dramatically as a result of the economic crisis that took hold in 2008.

In the midst of a deepening economic downturn, the Foundation Center has estimated that the nation's grantmaking foundations increased their giving 2.8 percent in 2008. Although this change amounted to a 1 percent decrease after inflation, foundation giving nonetheless remained remarkably stable given the severity of the downturn. Looking ahead, however, the Center expects that foundation giving will decrease in the range of the high single digits to low double digits in 2009 and decline further in 2010.[1]

What does this mean for social justice-related funding? Undoubtedly, grant dollars for social justice will decrease in the near term, as they will for all areas of activity. But there is no reason to expect that social justice-related grantmaking will be disproportionately affected by the crisis.

Supporting this conclusion are findings from a Foundation Center research advisory, which showed that the economic downturn of the early 2000s did not have a discernable impact on foundations' funding priorities.[2] Findings from an early 2009 survey buttress this conclusion, with the vast majority of foundation respondents reporting that they do not anticipate changing the number of program areas they currently support.[3] Moreover, given the recent change in administration in the United States and the impact of the economic crisis on already disadvantaged populations, there may be even greater incentive for foundations to seek opportunities to support social justice.

Endnotes

1. See Lawrence, S., and R. Mukai, *Foundation Growth and Giving Estimates: Current Outlook*, New York: Foundation Center, 2009.
2. See Lawrence, S., *Do Foundation Giving Priorities Change in Times of Economic Distress?*, New York: Foundation Center, 2008.
3. See Lawrence, S., *Foundations Address the Impact of the Economic Crisis*, New York: Foundation Center, 2009.

Introduction

By Bradford K. Smith

Social Justice Grantmaking II comes out at a time when a deep economic recession grips the world and poverty and vulnerability are on the rise. Arguably, American foundations, which saw a more than doubling of their collective assets over the 10 years preceding the recession, did not do enough to address persistent injustice, inequality, and discrimination when they had the means to do so. Now, despite an estimated 22 percent decline in their assets in 2008 alone, they have no choice but to do more.

The pages that follow give cause for optimism that foundations will rise to that challenge. Compared to 2005, when the Foundation Center released the first *Social Justice Grantmaking* study, social justice philanthropy is growing, is being practiced by more foundations, and is increasingly referred to as a "field." Some foundations, such as the Rosenberg and Marguerite Casey foundations, devote nearly all of their grantmaking to social justice work. Other grantmakers that support a wide range of causes, such as the W.K. Kellogg and Citi foundations, figure prominently in the study by virtue of the volume of their resources that support social justice-related activities.

Another indication that social justice philanthropy is here to stay is exemplified by two of the larger institutions making grants in America. The Atlantic Philanthropies recently recast its longstanding mission of fostering lasting changes in the lives of disadvantaged and vulnerable people into what its president, Gara LaMarche, calls "a vision of social justice" that pays "particular attention to people and groups who are systematically disadvantaged by social and economic barriers that result in injustice and inequity." Under the leadership of Luis Ubiñas, the Ford Foundation has announced that its programs will address "eight significant social justice issues," from "Human Rights" to "Economic Fairness and Opportunity." One of these core issues is specifically entitled "Social Justice Philanthropy," through which Ford is committed to strengthening "the role and effectiveness of philanthropy around the world on issues of fairness, equity, and justice."

This study will undoubtedly provoke its share of controversy, as did its predecessor. While the Foundation Center has taken a working definition of social justice philanthropy crafted by philanthropic leaders and applied it to a large set of objective data on foundation grantmaking, those who have identified themselves as social justice funders for many years might disagree with the inclusion of some foundations and grants. Likewise, those who do not explicitly describe what they do as furthering social justice may be surprised to see themselves alongside foundations that do. For example, the Bill & Melinda Gates Foundation, though it believes strongly that "all lives have equal value," does not frequently use the term "social justice" to describe

> "This study will undoubtedly provoke its share of controversy, as did its predecessor."

> "[This study] reminds us of the power of philanthropy to take on some of the most difficult challenges we face as a nation and as a global community."

its work. Nevertheless, Gates leads all social justice funders as measured by the volume of its giving—more than $350 million in 2006.

The purpose of this report is to illuminate the growing field of social justice philanthropy and bring concrete evidence to discussions of the field's role and value. It also reminds us of the power of philanthropy to take on some of the most difficult challenges we face as a nation and as a global community. We have the immense privilege to work in a sector where our job is to leave the world a far better place than we found it. The foundations portrayed in this study deserve our respect and gratitude for striving to do just that.

Benchmarking Social Justice Grantmaking

By Steven Lawrence

The process of benchmarking social justice grantmaking required the involvement of INDEPENDENT SECTOR, the Foundation Center, and a set of advisors. This chapter briefly documents the role of these participants in the original *Social Justice Grantmaking* project, highlights key elements of the new report, and presents the working definition of social justice philanthropy adopted for these studies.

DEFINITION AND MEASUREMENT

Prior to the publication of the original *Social Justice Grantmaking* study in 2005, there had been no quantitative measurement of social justice-related funding by U.S. private and community foundations. Anecdote provided the only means for understanding the dimensions of grantmaking for social justice and assessing how it was faring relative to overall foundation giving. The methodology established by that study for the first time enabled the field of philanthropy to examine in detail the priorities of social justice funders and benchmark changes in their support over time.

Establishing a protocol for measuring social justice grantmaking required the work of INDEPENDENT SECTOR (IS), the Foundation Center, and a set of advisors. IS convened an advisory committee to craft a definition of social justice philanthropy, and they ultimately adopted a slightly modified version of the definition created by the National Committee for Responsive Philanthropy (see "Social Justice Philanthropy: A Working Definition").

The Foundation Center joined the project to map the new definition of social justice philanthropy to actual grants awarded by foundations. Working with IS and the advisory committee, the Center applied the definition to the grants data it collects annually from a set of the largest U.S. foundations and codes according to the National Taxonomy of Exempt Entities and its Grants Classification System. (See appendixes A through C for additional details.) This entailed reviewing thousands of individual grant records to ensure the accuracy of the mapping and reviewing this process and related questions with project advisors.

This "mapping" captured the intent of the working definition in actual grants data and also provided an objective means for measuring social change funding. Because the classification system does not provide a means for capturing values-based grantmaking— e.g., the giving of a foundation that considers all of its funding to be social justice related—only grants that met the "objective" criteria established using the IS definition were included in the set. Of course, this meant that the social justice grantmaking of both "progressive" and "conservative" foundations was reflected in the analysis of giving trends. The definition also encompassed the grantmaking of foundations not typically considered to be active in social justice funding. Most importantly, it ensured that the Foundation Center would be able to provide consistent measurement of changes in social justice-related grantmaking going forward.

THE NEW REPORT

Consistent with the original project's goal of providing ongoing measurement of social justice philanthropy, in 2008 the Foundation Center began the process of updating the *Social Justice Grantmaking* study. The Center convened a group of advisors, including several of the advisors who participated on the original committee, to develop and review the content of the new report.

Among the many questions advisors addressed, arguably the most critical was whether to amend the working definition of social justice philanthropy adopted for the original study to make it either more or less inclusive. The advisors determined that, while aspects of the definition may generate debate, overall it continues to provide a reasonable representation of social justice grantmaking by U.S. foundations.

With the question of definition resolved, the advisory committee turned to the report's content and interpretations of findings. Based on their recommendations, the new study includes:

◆ An examination of critical ideas and questions identified by leading social justice funders and nonprofit leaders at the outset of a new generation of social justice philanthropy.

◆ A discussion of how some social justice organizations and grantmakers are now explicitly bringing human rights back into the domestic context.

◆ A detailed analysis of social justice-related grantmaking by U.S. private and community foundations through 2006, along with a brief examination of giving by a set of leading public foundations social justice funders.

These analyses and resources are intended to enhance the work of funders and organizations active in supporting social change for those least well off politically, economically, and socially. They also serve to help educate the public about the wide-ranging interests and priorities of foundations that support social justice-related activities. However, this report by no means captures all social justice-related funders or activities. Readers should be certain to seek out information provided directly by foundations active in social change funding for the most complete perspective on their grantmaking priorities.

SOCIAL JUSTICE PHILANTHROPY: A WORKING DEFINITION[1]

Social justice philanthropy is the granting of philanthropic contributions to nonprofit organizations based in the United States and other countries that work for structural change in order to increase the opportunity of those who are the least well off politically, economically, and socially. It includes the following broad categories of activity:

◆ **Researching root causes of social problems such as poverty, discrimination, health care disparities, and lack of access to the political process, public policymaking, and economic opportunity.**

◆ **Communicating and disseminating this information to the public, with a particular emphasis on reaching those who are directly affected by social problems.**

◆ **Strengthening new and/or existing social movements that work for social, political, and economic equity through:**

· Grassroots activism to mobilize disadvantaged and disenfranchised groups;

· Creating networks or alliances among social justice groups;

· Community organizing toward increasing opportunity and redistributing socioeconomic power;

· Capacity building for nonprofits working toward social justice, including activities such as the enhancement of board development, inclusion of constituencies in decision making, and promotion of democratic funding processes;

· Economic development that increases the rights, opportunities, and financial stability of disadvantaged and disenfranchised groups;

· Health system change that increases access to health care and addresses disparities in the availability and quality of care for disadvantaged and disenfranchised groups;

· Educational reform that addresses inequities in access to and the quality of education for disadvantaged and disenfranchised groups;

· Labor organizing that increases the rights and opportunities of disadvantaged and disenfranchised groups;

· Environmental causes that ensure that disadvantaged groups are not disproportionately affected by harmful environmental practices;

· Peace and reconciliation programs that seek to understand and address the causes of conflict; and

· Advocacy and lobbying to enact changes in government policies, regulations, and programs affecting disadvantaged populations.

◆ **Protecting and enhancing the legal rights of those who are marginalized in society or discriminated against.**

Endnote

1. Prepared by INDEPENDENT SECTOR and the *Social Justice Grantmaking* advisory committee.

 Social Justice Philanthropy for a New Era

By Scott Nielsen, Ph.D., and Henry A.J. Ramos

Following years of declining faith in the efficacy of social justice philanthropy, both grantmakers and advocates are showing renewed optimism. Yet this growing confidence in the potential of social justice work is accompanied by a willingness to rethink earlier efforts and identify the strategies that promise the greatest chance of success going forward. Based on interviews with a selection of leading social justice funders and nonprofit leaders, this chapter identifies critical ideas and questions at the outset of a new generation of social justice philanthropy.

INTRODUCTION

At the beginning of the 21st century, American society finds itself in circumstances that are both dramatically new and distressingly familiar. Economic globalization, new technology and the Internet, and increasing multicultural harmony and progress are changing the way we live and work, and are improving the well-being of many Americans. On the other hand, worsening income inequality, the decline of pillar institutions, and increased environmental stress are creating social and economic injury and marginalization that in turn promote ongoing unfairness and need.

Despite these challenges, funders and advocates are more positive about the prospects for social justice philanthropy to have a meaningful impact than was true just a few years ago. In our 2005 interview study with leading social justice grantmakers, we found many to be pessimistic and frustrated, with a number of funders questioning the very salience of social justice as a phrase, concept, and operating strategy.[1] Many respondents described proponents of social justice as operating with dated agendas and strategies that had grown incoherent or off-putting to other segments of U.S. society—including mainstream philanthropy. Some foundations looked to the private sector to find functional strategies and partnerships that did not begin with the traditional assumptions, constituencies, and ideologies of social justice.

Three years later, we conducted interviews with 18 leading social justice funders and grantmaker affinity groups and eight social justice advocates to determine how the field may have changed. Among the most notable changes, the majority of funders we interviewed for this updated study would readily define their work as social justice philanthropy. Following the 2006 elections, and especially with the Obama candidacy and election, social justice funders and advocates have developed a renewed optimism about the future of social justice grantmaking. Nonetheless, both foundations and advocates in the field are bringing a critical eye to past efforts as they seek to identify the strategies that will work best to promote social justice in the current environment. For example, the recent demise of the National Network of Grantmakers, the affinity group most directly serving social justice funders, signaled "the end of the social justice movement that dominated the field for 25 years," said one funder. "Something new and more flexible is forming to take up this work. It's an exciting time."

Interviewees offered perspectives on the past as well as ideas for moving the social justice field forward. It should be noted that the recommendations offered throughout this essay belong to the funders and advocates themselves. We recognize that different institutions, on-the-ground situations, and social justice visions will use different approaches and strategies to make change.

THE FUNDER PERSPECTIVE

Social justice philanthropy promotes the structural reform of institutions and public policies that tend to generate inequality and unfairness. Most social justice funders orient their grantmaking around constituencies or issues—such as youth, people of color, the environment, housing, or health care—and their work encompasses a broad array of strategies, social networks, and policy objectives. A few foundations support specific strategies that impact many constituencies and issues, such as litigation, movement building, or the creation and nurturing of multi-issue and multi-constituency coalitions.

Although social justice grantmakers bring diverse perspectives to their work, interviews with a group of 18 leading private and public social justice funders and affinity groups revealed broad agreement about where the field of social justice philanthropy has been successful and areas where funders should focus their work going forward. (See page iv for a complete list of participating institutions.) The following sections identify a series of strategies and practices suggested by interviewees for advancing the work of social justice philanthropy.

Adopt a "Small Tent" Strategy

In the past, many multi-issue and multi-constituency collaborations, usually at the state or metropolitan level, sought to enroll an expansive organizational and stakeholder base— sometimes at funders' insistence. These "big-tent" collaboratives included every group, often regardless of scale, in the region that was interested in a social justice agenda. This logic held that "the bigger the group, the bigger the impact, and the bigger the funder pool." However, these large collaborations could be contentious and have difficulty moving quickly. Often "they consumed a lot of time, and yielded very little social change," said one funder. "The stronger groups dictated strategy and the smaller, less well-resourced groups were either excluded or superfluous."

In rethinking this strategy, both funders and advocates identified a growing trend toward "small tent" collaborations, which contain fewer groups, and are seen to be more nimble and disciplined, and provide a higher level of trust and mutual accountability. The rise during the 2008 election of "501(c)(3) tables" is a successful example of this innovation, and a promising model for issue and constituency organizing and advocacy. Groups like State Voices and the Pushback Network convened and provided technical assistance to these networks or tables of local and state multi-issue groups working together during the election on nonprofit voter projects.

Find Common Ground

Many funders we interviewed believe that social justice philanthropy is most effective when it seeks to bridge differences of race, class, language, region, and generation toward a vision of a common ground. For example, one health care funder noted that, "Our work…is positioning us more and more around racial disparities and workforce diversity issues, as people of color are especially challenged by structural impediments to [securing] equitable health care protection and industry representation." Other promising areas for bringing together multiple constituencies are economic development, political enfranchisement, education, and environmental concerns.

Focus on the Grassroots

A central tenet of social justice work, confirmed by our interviews, holds that social change is most relevant and lasting when it emanates from the ground up. Many believe that social justice work often fails when it is undertaken by intermediaries— however well meaning—outside of the community. By working with grassroots community groups and then their partners at state and national levels, policy priorities are inaugurated and sustained by the people most affected by them.

Community organizing continues to be the most prevalent grassroots social justice strategy, as it has been since the 1960s. But some place-based foundations have also been working with a variety of local agents to develop community wealth and other assets of power and influence. The goal of this work is not only to assist marginalized people in gaining access to mainstream resources, but also to help them generate those resources on their own. "Our mission is to move people out of poverty," said one funder. "This requires a comprehensive approach that builds on multiple intervention strategies…[both] 'above the line'–increasing community assets, improving living conditions, etc.—and 'below the line'— supporting policy change, enhancing community leadership, community organizing, etc."

Yet most interviewees cited community organizing as specifically and urgently underfunded. Some grantmakers noted that support for organizing never came back after the turn away from social justice grantmaking that was captured in our 2005 report. One foundation executive noted, "Community organizing is underfunded because it creates social change, [which] is inherently uncomfortable to some people." Another executive agreed, "This is a huge problem since civic engagement is such a bedrock of democracy…. Sadly, foundation culture does not like to address controversy, and still too many funders shy away from advocacy and organizing because they fear it will drive them away from their comfort zones."

Other interviewees believe that organizing as a field and strategy itself is in a period of transition, and that funding will return when it adapts to

new circumstances. "Most community organizing I see seems ineffective," said one funder. "The rhetoric is tired and the accomplishments seem small and few. The [organizing] groups themselves are often weak and tend to recycle the same 'power analysis' that ensures they and their community stakeholders will continue to be outsiders." Another funder believes that successful organizing groups must update and "use multiple approaches to promote change, including integrated voter engagement, youth leadership, legal advocacy, idea generation, policy change, and deployment of new technologies."

Do Not Ignore the Political Sphere

Although grassroots funding is the priority for social justice philanthropists, some funders note that grassroots support alone rarely yields enough political leverage and expertise to significantly address larger social justice issues. For these grantmakers, providing support for nonpartisan electoral and public sector participation is equally critical. One long-time social justice funder summarized the mission and vision of many funders in commenting that, "We support the pieces of infrastructure necessary for low-income people and people of color to be heard in policy decisions that affect their lives. These pieces include organizing and base-building, research and media, support to intermediaries that are genuine partners with community-based organizations, and community and organizational leadership. Overall, we seek to develop political clout, since that's where change happens most efficiently."

Support Identity-based Philanthropies

Interviewees agreed that the social justice sector as a whole is underfunded, but highlighted identity-based foundations as a promising source of new philanthropy. Women's donor groups have led this

"Organizing as a field and strategy itself is in a period of transition, and…funding will return when it adapts to new circumstances. 'Most community organizing I see seems ineffective,' said one funder."

> "Grantmakers named greater field cohesion and partnership as the second–greatest social justice priority...'We are too fractured as a field. We need to build on a common vision that leads to a more productive alignment of resources and strategies.' "

movement for 20 years, but new donors of color, LGBT donors, and others are increasingly organizing their community giving to promote social and economic progress in their communities. Larger private foundations, such as the Ford Foundation, W.K. Kellogg Foundation, and the California Endowment have been instrumental in supporting this growing philanthropic sector. Beyond increasing the resources available for social justice philanthropy, these identity-based institutions will also change the leadership, discourses, and grantmaking practices of social change advocacy.

Build and Renew the Social Justice Infrastructure

The importance of supporting an *infrastructure* that sustains and links the work of social justice organizations and grantmakers was referenced by several interviewees. Funders are increasingly supporting ongoing collaboration among national policy groups and their allies working for change at the state and local level. One interviewee summarized the view of many funders: "For a long time our sector has been too segmented; it's dysfunctional. The good work and leaders of national groups rarely meet the good work and leaders of community-based organizations. They don't understand each other. We need to build intermediary organizations and opportunities that network this field leadership and utilize the full range of social justice capacity." Another funder added, "To achieve their goals, most social justice groups must be accountable to a base, usually a community base. But grassroots groups usually cannot effect major change on their own. They need the resources—policy, media, funding, capacity building, partnerships—of other groups to gain power."

Additionally, multi-issue funders have coordinated with one another, often through funder affinity groups, to

support different facets of the social justice infrastructure. Funders appear to be more inclined than in the past to work across strategy or constituency. "Partnering with other foundations to leverage resources and help sustain organizations over the long term has been one of the most successful strategies we've seen."

There is also a growing consensus among funders—and grantee leaders— that the fields of technical assistance and organizational development need to be expanded and updated. "I look for organizational development consultants of color, or bilingual and bicultural technical assistance providers and have not had much luck," said one funder who works in the immigration field. Another donor wondered whether "the nonprofit sector is tapping the best organizational development thinking and innovative program designs used in the business and other sectors. Successful companies always invest in new ways to improve their productivity and staff capacity, why don't we?"

Collaborate with Other Funders

Grantmakers named greater field cohesion and partnership as the second-greatest social justice priority, behind the need for more core social justice funding. "We are too fractured as a field. We need to build on a common vision that leads to a more productive alignment of resources and strategies." In this way, funders are making demands of themselves similar to those they are making of grantees.

The increased desire for opportunities to network, convene, and collaborate is being sustained in part by new technology that is offering cost-effective ways to undertake peer learning and gain ongoing value from learning communities and other networks. Shared learning sites, webinars, streaming video, and other social networking vehicles promise rapid development of this field-building investment.

Collaborate with Grantees

The move toward closer collaboration is extending to the relationships between funders and their grantees as well. "It is incumbent on us to bridge the giver-recipient divide," said one senior foundation executive. "Of course, there are real power differentials that we have to be honest about and attentive to…but at the end of the day we are working toward the same vision."

Some funders are already making this level of collaboration core to their institutional strategy and operation. "We seek partnership, knowing the relationship will be messy. The key is to have open communication and to be evaluating *how* the partnership is going, to…take the time to build trust, to strive for transparency, and to hold each other accountable for results. Each side has a stake in the outcome." The grantmaker went on to note that this will require foundations to move beyond annual and project-specific funding, so that organizations can feel comfortable discussing their "real-time needs and vulnerabilities…so that together we can jump on opportunities and also deal with challenges and crises expediently."

To make these collaborations work, grantees need to be open to change and experimentation. The relationship will extend beyond "signing a grant check," commented one funder. "We've been surprised at how difficult it has been for some social justice groups to have a forthcoming and mutually accountable relationship with a funder. On the other hand, where it has worked, it has transformed both the foundation and the grantee group."

Another funder doubts that collaboration will develop into a sector-wide priority without a formal initiative. "We are simply too dichotomized, and the cost of this disassociation is very high. We need a social justice forum to help this happen—someplace where we could all come together and

encourage strategic collaboration and coordination." Several funders said this is already happening through funder affinity groups and other collaborations. For example, the *State Funders Group*, a subcommittee of the Funders' Committee on Civic Participation, gathers foundation and field leaders to collectively coordinate strategy and resource provision. The Four Freedoms Fund is a donor collaborative that funds immigration reform and human rights efforts. The Diversity in Philanthropy Project is a volunteer cohort of major foundation executives and trustees working to generate greater inclusion of diverse perspectives, talent, and experience in their institutions.

Funders also note an interesting cultural shift resulting from the generational transition happening in nonprofit leadership. "Our foundation has long urged social justice groups to collaborate on campaigns and issues of common concern, but without much success," said one grantmaker. "Competition for authority, funding scarcity, and a general territoriality has often made genuine partnership difficult. However, among younger leaders I am finding exactly the reverse. They prefer working with and learning from allies, sharing resources, and they have the sense that collaboration is efficient and achieves scale. This is hopeful."

Create Capacity

Not surprisingly, all of the social justice funders we interviewed agreed that making general support grants to premier groups—multi-year if possible—constitutes the ideal funding strategy. Less expected was the rising commitment among these grantmakers to capacity building as a way to strengthen organizations, the field, and prospects for sustained social change. This enthusiasm comes with a growing recognition that funders are asking both too much and too little of their grantees.

"This enthusiasm [for capacity building] comes with a growing recognition that funders are asking both too much and too little of their grantees."

> "Some social justice funders also find the growing use of evaluations to be counter-productive...'Real change requires more than a grant cycle or two to achieve.' "

On the one hand, grantmakers establish expectations for innovation and success that are not buttressed with the resources necessary to make groups capable of meeting these expectations. As one long-time funder of community-based organizations noted, "Capacity building gives you the biggest bang for the buck. But this support has to be more than $5,000 for a five-year strategic plan—which often yields little except a thick document."

On the other hand, some nonprofits are simply underperforming and will not achieve the desired scale regardless of capacity-building investments. "I've had a strong critique of the social change organizational sector for its frequent lack of professionalism, lack of attention paid to effective organizational management, failure to modernize strategically and tactically, inability to develop and sustain new leaders—especially people of color—and what I feel is too much indulgence of feel-good, well-intentioned mediocrity. After all, if the organizations that we invest in are not able to 'deliver the goods' of meaningful and lasting policy and community changes for the people and communities who are counting on them, then this work is just not working."

Most grantmakers share this interest in making organizations stronger—both small, community-based organizations and national anchor groups. The preferred capacity-building investment among current funders is leadership development, usually for grantees' executive directors and, occasionally, promising community members. Sometimes this leadership development is purely skill building. In other instances, leadership development is geared more toward leaders' self-actualization and the notion of leaders as agents of social change. Indeed, foundation executives themselves are building their own leadership capacities through the Rockwood Leadership Program and other providers.

Plan for a New Generation of Leadership

Most funders acknowledged the social justice field is at the beginning of a large leadership transition, as baby boomer executives retire. Foundations are increasingly focusing on the development of young leaders to build the bench that will run important nonprofits in years to come. Yet senior leaders are often not ready or able to move on. "Simply put, we have many long-time leaders with great expertise, relationships, and historic knowledge who are holding on [to their positions] feeling that there is no place for them to go [professionally] and still be rooted in this work. We also have many dynamic, diverse, and talented young leaders, especially from people of color communities, who feel like there is no commitment to building a pipeline for new leaders and that organizational structures are built more for the 1970s than 2009." On the other hand, many new leaders come into groups from outside the organization and the field. Because they were never deputies or never had hands-on training and experience, their learning curve is extremely steep. Many burn out after a few years. Consequently, "there must be a greater commitment to investing in leadership development pipelines, from entry-level on-ramps to succession planning for existing, long-time leaders."

Another donor agreed, noting that, "Funders have not used their role to encourage succession planning and other measures of organizational and field stewardship. We need to think about career paths for mid-career and senior nonprofit leaders. We need to create places for them to go and thrive, earn a salary and continue to share their expertise with the field. By focusing only on young people, we set them up for frustration, and we might neglect a key asset [senior leaders] in whom we have invested year after year." Negotiating this leadership transition and next-generation development will be a central piece of social justice organization over the next decade.

Re-evaluate the Role of Evaluation

Numerous funders now routinely ask for an evaluation plan as a part of their grant agreements, and many hire consultants to assess the outcome of their investments. This requirement has been controversial in the social justice field, generally resulting from a lack of agreed-upon indices of success and accomplishment, especially quantitative analyses. Some social justice funders also find the growing use of evaluations to be counter-productive. As one interviewee remarked, "We need to de-emphasize the field's recent over-concern about things like 'success' and 'innovation'…. We need to be more realistic about what real change requires and how much we can influence it. Impact is not a bad thing to measure, but context is also important. Real change requires more than a grant cycle or two to achieve."

A number of funders said that the lack of clear protocols to measure social justice progress and impact creates problems for both funders and their grantees. "We never settled on adequate metrics for issue-based advocacy work," remarked one interviewee. This work "doesn't lend itself to numbers the way direct service work does, for example." But some grantmakers were willing to show flexibility, including a grantmaker who commented, "We do not want grantees to feel they are being judged through evaluations. It is a learning tool for us and for them. If there are weaknesses or gaps, we can address them together."

Despite these challenges, most funders believe that evaluation is necessary and useful. "We need to know what is working and what is not. And if we can, let's find out why some practice is working, and see if it can be replicated elsewhere. Then we can synthesize and disseminate the research and evidence in a way that makes it compelling for policymakers. And where we discover activities that do not work, let's adapt."

Embrace Mission-related Investing

Some foundations are using program-related investments and mission-driven investments to augment their grant support for community groups. In the past, these partnerships with business and public sector allies might not have been considered social justice philanthropy at all, since they involve cooperation with sectors often seen as opponents of the priorities of marginalized groups. However, this worldview is changing. As one funder noted bluntly, "To gain power it is useful to work with those who already have it." This shift in attitude and calculation suggests a growing domain within social justice philanthropy that relies less on the "politics of confrontation," as one funder put it, and more on pragmatic partnerships that promote an increasingly ecumenical vision of the common good.

Target Underfunded Priorities

Community organizing ranked at the top of interviewees' lists of under-funded activities within the social justice field. Other areas of activity grantmakers considered to be under-funded included communications and the use of technology, youth and people of color leadership development, mid-career leadership development, convening and collaboration, and technical assistance dedicated specifically to sustain networks and collaborations.

Funders were in even greater agreement about social justice fields that seem over-funded. In the minds of many interviewees, national think tank and policy groups, often based in Washington, DC, receive a disproportionate share of foundation funding. "These groups have no legs whatsoever in communities," said one grantmaker. "Also these organizations are usually not led by people of color." Some interviewees believe that foundation affinity groups receive too much support, although

"Many of the organization leaders interviewed believe that progressives have yet to put forth an updated and broadly compelling vision of the common good."

others identified grantmaker affinity groups and funder collaboratives as being among the most successful social justice initiatives they know, with a high return on investment.

THE PRACTITIONER PERSPECTIVE

All social justice practitioners interviewed for this study agree that the fields of social change activism and advocacy are evolving rapidly to accommodate new technologies, strategies, tactics, issues, and constituencies. Many interviewees also believe that social justice activism is likely entering a period of renewal after a long retrenchment. "The Reagan era put social change organizations on the defensive, and they were unable to respond effectively to the government's disinvestment from public programs for low-income Americans," said a long-time organizer. "As a result, our organizations focused on smaller and smaller issues, meaning our leverage to make change almost disappeared beyond the neighborhood level." Another practitioner noted that "beginning in the 1980s, the moral case, which always fueled successful social justice…lost its currency and force with the broader public."

Many of the organization leaders interviewed believe that progressives have yet to put forth an updated and broadly compelling vision of the common good. But starting in the early 2000s, social justice advocates changed their strategies in two significant ways that might remedy this gap. First, many more social justice groups became involved in electoral politics. "We need to make our politics more like our population," said one leader. "Social justice comes through interaction with government. The policies that promote social justice can be had only through electoral engagement. To eschew politics is to forfeit the surest path to power, and hence to justice and equality." Another organization head

added, "I can't imagine we'll stay out of electoral politics in the way we had before 2004. We've had success, which is always motivating, and we learned new skills and strategies. Elections energize our base in ways no other campaigns can."

Second, social justice organizations have increasingly focused on communications, messaging, and media relations to build their base and educate the public and decision makers. "We learned from the Right that public opinion, even at the community level, was set through the media, and yet we were not challenging our adversaries or putting forth our arguments in that way. Once we became sophisticated at communicating through earned and paid media, our constituencies became more sophisticated, and public officials more attentive. We were defining ourselves and our agenda rather than being defined by opponents."

According to one executive director, these two shifts "are helping to transform organizing into a position of negotiation, and away from a purely adversarial stance. Permanent polarization and opposition is boring and ineffectual; we were losing our campaigns and our community backing." Instead, "we are now redefining our path to influence. We are asking our stakeholders and ourselves how we enroll bigger alliances and approach power not as a tactic but as an organizing frame. Start with the cookie, not with the crumbs."

Many interviewees believe that the Obama victory will produce a seismic shift in the social justice field. "The discipline and sophistication [of the Obama campaign] as a community organizing event demonstrates what is possible when organizing is adequately funded, technologically equipped, and rhetorically sound," remarked one leader. "It has both affirmed the power and legitimacy of community organizing as a force for social justice, and also puts into relief the uneven current state of the community organizing field."

This positive energy has combined with a frank assessment of past practices that did not help to advance social justice. "We have been too insular, reactive, and resistant to change," said one organizer. "We have been somewhat anti-intellectual," said another, "with a romantic notion of an organic, grassroots, street knowledge that is more authentic than academic or policy research. This is changing now, but we have resisted intellectuals for 20 years."

Beyond assessing how their own work is being transformed in the current environment, the eight social justice organization leaders interviewed for this report identified several ways that funders could enhance their support for this work. (See page iv for a complete list of participating institutions.) Following are their recommendations.

Engage in Strategic Partnerships

Social justice practitioners have mixed thoughts about their funders and about the relationship between the grantee and grantmaker. On the one hand, practitioners feel that closer partnership is possible with grantmakers in ways it has never been before. Some funders regard social justice leaders as trusted strategy partners, whose insights inform the mission and work of social justice foundations. Increasingly foundations invite community leaders and organization executives onto their boards and program committees. Many program officers help raise money for their leading grantees, and find ways to promote sector leaders. The line between those having funds and those requesting funds never disappears altogether, but in many instances the strategic partnership is close to one of peers.

On the other hand, the divide between funders and practitioners continues to limit field growth and experimentation. "Foundations still seem timid and risk averse," said one social justice leader. "We need more forums for honest joint exchange," said another activist. "Every time we have the opportunity to engage funders in a meaningful way, we've been successful in getting support." Advocates stress that this is not a request for more show-and-tell conferences, which most feel is a waste of time. Rather, they seek a qualitatively different encounter— one of trust, directness, and honesty.

Support Community Organizing and Other Underfunded Activities

Consistent with the perspective of grantmakers, practitioners too believe that high-quality community organizing is underfunded and undervalued by philanthropy. Interviewees also believe that civic engagement and election-related activities are underfunded. In light of recent electoral advances, one leader remarked, "The success of 2008 will lead many groups to become more involved politically to increase impact. But will funders support this?" Other underfunded activities cited by practitioners include leadership development, litigation, coalition building, investment in rural social justice, and work that builds a global social justice movement.

In thinking about the range of needs in the field, one leader summarized the view of many in asking, "Is social justice philanthropy thinking about the field as a field, with structural and alignment needs? In some ways, philanthropy's segmentation in terms of interests and guidelines has created a fractured field. If funders thought more holistically, we could together determine the resource needs more easily and address them. This is especially pressing given our economic situation."

"The line between those having funds and those requesting funds never disappears altogether, but in many instances the strategic partnership is close to one of peers."

> "[Practitioners] are not opposed to effective evaluation efforts. 'Often the best groups are not encouraged to pursue their best ideas, and weak groups are allowed to limp along. Raise the bar!' "

Provide Multi-year, Unrestricted Support

All of the practitioners interviewed for this study agreed that the way foundation grants are typically made inhibits the field. "One-year project grants encourage small, tentative work and are caustic to bold and innovative thinking," said a coalition leader. "Multi-year, general support grants are the most efficient way to encourage innovation and creativity. Especially when a group has been a grantee year after year, it drains energy and resources to force them to re-up every 12 months."

Fund Constructive Evaluation Efforts

While practitioners may at times feel burdened by current efforts at evaluating their work, they are not opposed to effective evaluation efforts. "Often the best groups are not encouraged to pursue their best ideas, and weak groups are allowed to limp along. Raise the bar!" said one leader. Another interviewee agreed, "So much [social change work] is unaccountable and yet is funded year after year. Developing proper metrics to demonstrate success is a moral and strategic necessity for our fields. It will become clear which groups deserve increased resources."

Connect Think Tanks, Intermediaries, and Small Community-based Organizations

When asked for their perspective on over-funded social justice activities, practitioners cited similar and sometimes conflicting ideas. Like social justice funders, most social justice groups believe that national think tanks and policy groups receive disproportionately high levels of funding relative to their impact. "We see the value of this work in developing and moving policy," said

one advocate. "We should be allies, but these institutions are rarely connected to advocacy or other grassroots groups. And every year there seem to be more DC-centered think tanks soaking up more funding. Who's their base?"

"We have too many intermediaries," said another organizer. "Suddenly big foundations are cutting ties to grassroots groups and preferring to pass large amounts of funding through intermediaries who are rarely accountable to the base they were set up to support. Instead, they are accountable only to funders. They also become gatekeepers so that funders and national allies learn about the grassroots only from intermediaries, who often don't understand grassroots realities, and are naturally self-interested. I understand the need of large foundations to find creative ways to make small grants, but this rise of intermediaries is not healthy."

On the other hand, some social justice practitioners believe too many small-issue and -constituency groups are being supported, especially in crowded geographies. "I think we can agree that, with a few exceptions, small community-based organizations have very limited impact in promoting significant social change. They are not connected to state, regional, and national allies. Sometimes there are several tiny groups working on the same issue in a single city or region. Why can't they join together to build scale, expertise, and impact?"

The recent economic downturn may hasten the contraction of the social justice field. "There will be some shakeout," said one executive director. "Funders will be making some life-and-death decisions when they make grants, and many small community-based organizations will either consolidate with larger groups, or will disappear. This might not be an altogether bad thing."

THE FUTURE OF SOCIAL JUSTICE PHILANTHROPY

Most social justice funders are optimistic about the future of the sector, and about the efficacy of social justice advocacy as a vehicle for social change. A large measure of this optimism is fueled by recent electoral victories—both national and in key states—and the success of public sector leaders who have spoken of reinstating a social contract that would enroll government in redressing social and economic unfairness and inequality.

Funders also see a growing sophistication in some sectors of the social justice infrastructure. This includes not only greater fluency with technology and a willingness to partner widely, but also a new ideology and language. Today's social justice leaders "are shifting away from identity politics," said one funder. "We are a country of growing and divergent inequalities and we need a new universal." Another funder noticed a similar trend in the way social justice foundations are defining their programs. Funders are choosing "to ensure more focus on human rights as opposed to civil rights…[which] may broaden the constituency for change and also the stakeholders who feel compelled to support the work." (See Chapter 3, "The Return to Human Rights," for a more detailed discussion of this trend.)

Leading social justice funders and their grantees continue to view communities as the vanguard of progress and authentic reform. In this way, the discourses and policy priorities of social justice philanthropy are not substantively different than they have been for a decade. Yet grantmakers are now thinking again about movement building and infrastructure and the totality of resources and capacities required to gain and sustain public policies that promote a broad public interest agenda. They also seem to be focusing more on structure and process than on program and ideology.

The challenge created by this optimism is whether the social justice field, which for so long has been outside the circles of power, can move rapidly enough to be a conduit and steward of power, policy, innovation, and resources. "We must quickly confront a social justice organizational culture that is comfortable being oppositional but has not given attention to thinking about how to govern. My hunch and fear is that many of our grantees know better how to exist and prioritize work when [their adversaries] are in power." This strategic shift from opposition to governing will be the central social justice challenge moving forward.

For their part, social justice practitioners also see the field as being in a period of rapid change and wonder whether funders can move swiftly and strategically enough to join them in creating the next stage of nonprofit social justice advocacy. Practitioners feel that this is more possible now than before, especially given the opportunities afforded by the Obama presidency. But the gloomy economic forecast and some foundations' resistance to change give them concern.

For both grantmakers and practitioners, the social justice field's next stage will require a broader array of programs and strategies and must appeal to a wider cross-section of Americans. "The last 25 years have taught us that we need a more expansive message and course of action," said on long-time funder. "Speaking confrontational truth to power no longer works, if it ever did. Power has no trouble ignoring or punishing us. We have to be more sophisticated analysts of social, economic, and political trends. I think the past two years and the impressive electoral work our sector has undertaken proves it's possible. Now we have to consider what's next."

ENDNOTE

1. See Foundation Center, *Social Justice Grantmaking: A Report on Foundation Trends*, edited by S. Lawrence, New York: Foundation Center, 2005.

> " 'The last 25 years have taught us that we need a more expansive message and course of action. Speaking confrontational truth to power no longer works, if it ever did. Power has no trouble ignoring or punishing us.' "

The Return to Human Rights

By Tanya E. Coke[1]

For at least 50 years, a clear distinction was made been made between civil rights and social justice issues in the United States and efforts to ensure human rights globally. Some social justice organizations and grantmakers are now explicitly bringing human rights back into the domestic context. To understand the factors motivating this change and challenges to its broad acceptance, this chapter documents findings based on interviews with a selection of U.S.-based social justice funders and nonprofit leaders.

CHANGING PERCEPTIONS

A major reproductive rights group changes its mission to include reference to human rights. The largest civil liberties organization in the United States establishes a human rights program. Three advocacy networks are founded since 1998 to focus on domestic human rights. Over 140 domestic social justice activists draft a report to the United Nations and travel to Geneva to demand that the United States be held accountable for addressing racial injustice at home. A shift in the perceived relevance of human rights to the domestic civil rights and social justice arena is clearly underway—but what factors are driving this change?

For most of the 20th century, social justice advocacy in the United States meant working to ensure civil rights. Much of this work was undertaken by women activists and African Americans in their struggle to win political rights to the franchise and social rights to participate as full members of society, as well as by those seeking equal protections for LGBT populations, the disabled, and other marginalized groups. Human rights, by contrast, was generally perceived as referring to the struggles of political dissidents enduring repressive regimes in faraway places, like China and the Soviet Union.

Rights work was not always so divided. In 1947, following a devastating world war and the genocide of millions of Jews in Europe, Eleanor Roosevelt and a team of world leaders gathered to draft the Universal Declaration of Human Rights (UDHR). The authors agreed on the central importance of affirming universal respect for human rights and fundamental freedoms, including the principles of non-discrimination and political rights. They also identified social, cultural, and economic rights, such as the right to have an adequate standard of living, access education, and seek asylum. These rights were not rooted in the laws of any one country but in the very fact of being human. As the UDHR preamble declared, its purpose was to ensure that all people had "rights indispensable for the dignity and development of the human personality."

Chief among Roosevelt's domestic advisors in this effort were major figures of the civil rights era, including W.E.B. DuBois and Walter White of the NAACP. These civil rights activists viewed the UDHR as a potentially powerful tool to end lynching and Jim Crow segregation in the United States. They also saw within the human rights framework the opportunity to redress substandard education, health care, and housing for black Americans.

But their segregationist opponents grasped the potential of human rights, too. Aided by Secretary of State John Foster Dulles, a bloc of southern senators effectively thwarted U.S. implementation of the UDHR and subsequent international human rights treaties. Civil rights leaders and those who supported a global vision of human rights were labeled communists, traitors, and worse. Under the withering assault of Cold War politics, the domestic movement to engage with international human rights eventually died, even as that same framework gave rise to an extensive system of human rights laws

> "Human rights...was generally perceived as referring to the struggles of political dissidents enduring repressive regimes in faraway places."

and tribunals actively used by other nations around the world.

As a result, a bifurcated landscape of rights advocacy prevailed in the United States for the next 50 years: human rights applied elsewhere—as a shaming tool to criticize the practices of our country's ideological foes—while civil rights applied at home. In the 1970s and 1980s, U.S.-based human rights organizations, such as Human Rights Watch (formerly Helsinki Watch), Amnesty International, the Lawyer's Committee for Human Rights (now Human Rights First), and the International Human Rights Lawyer Group (now Global Rights), emerged and prospered. But these human rights defenders focused their work on abuses occurring in foreign countries.

A NEW GENERATION TAKES UP HUMAN RIGHTS

Six decades after the creation of the Universal Declaration of Human Rights, there appears to be a return to a more integrated perspective on civil and human rights within the United States. A stronger embrace of human rights framing among grassroots organizations and an increased interest in international legal standards among lawyers point toward this trend. To explore the extent of this shift and the factors driving the change, we interviewed several grantmakers and their grantees about how social justice and human rights framing evolved and is currently being viewed.

Alan Jenkins, executive director of The Opportunity Agenda—a communications think tank—and former program director at the Ford Foundation, sees a definite trend toward human rights framing. He noted that, "Over the past decade there has been a substantive shift in both terminology and approach. Social justice groups realized that the dominant anti-discrimination protections were falling short of what's

needed. Often human rights treaties offer more effective approaches." Gara LaMarche, president and CEO of Atlantic Philanthropies, agreed that, "The framework of human rights for change is a quite genuine trend. In the last five or 10 years, there is something on the ground that is real and has begun to affect the more established international and national mainstream human rights groups. Grantmakers have taken the lead in recognizing this trend—I would place the Ford Foundation at the head of this pack—but have also been pushed and educated by the field."

Some of the earliest activists to take up international human rights were Native American tribes, which have used their status as sovereign nations to advocate for land and cultural rights at the United Nations and other international tribunals. But several people pointed to the international women's rights conference in Beijing in 1995 and the 2001 international race conference in Durban, South Africa, as catalyzing events in the rebirth of domestic human rights. "In Beijing, 'women's rights are human rights' was the pervasive theme," noted Betsy Brill, executive director of the Libra Foundation and president of Strategic Philanthropy, Ltd., a philanthropic advisory firm. "Hundreds of women from the U.S. were at that meeting." These activists saw a global landscape of women using a common language of dignity and equality to describe their goals and employing international human rights standards, like the Convention on the Elimination of Discrimination Against Women (CEDAW), to agitate for change. Around the same time, international human rights organizations like Global Rights, Human Rights Watch, and Amnesty International began to develop U.S. programs that focused on domestic civil rights issues, like policing, felon disenfranchisement, and prison conditions, through a human rights lens.

In 2002, a diverse group of U.S. advocates and scholars from the women's rights, racial justice, and economic rights movements met at Howard University and resolved to form a national human rights network. In 2004, the U.S. Human Rights Network launched with 50 organizational members. Today the Network has grown to 280 members and includes grassroots as well as large legal and policy groups, like the American Civil Liberties Union, the Brennan Center at New York University, the Lawyers' Committee for Civil Rights Under Law, and the NAACP Legal Defense Fund.

GRANTMAKERS RESPOND TO A SHIFTING LANDSCAPE

Before 1995, the Ford Foundation was organized like most other international foundations: it had a U.S. division, which focused on civil rights, and international field offices, which addressed human rights overseas. Larry Cox, director of Amnesty International USA, staffed the human rights portfolio during that period. "When I first began working at the Ford Foundation in 1995, the human rights program officer was located in the International Affairs Department and had little contact with the Rights and Social Justice Department, which is where U.S. work was done. When I began trying to organize funding support at Ford and with other grantmakers for human rights work in the United States, some of the strongest opposition came from the most progressive foundations. They were able to cite numerous civil rights and social justice grantees who agreed that, whatever the demonstrated power of human rights to transform other societies, in this one the language, methodologies, and the idea of human rights would at best not help and at worst would harm the fight here."

Nevertheless, in response to what Ford saw as a nascent interest in human rights at home, Cox hired Dorothy

Thomas, an early advocate of "bringing human rights home," to design a series of donor roundtables to explore the emerging movement around human rights. The work culminated in a 2003 conference and publication entitled, *Close to Home: Case Studies of Human Rights Work in the U.S.* As a direct outcome of this work, 10 grantmakers launched the U.S. Human Rights Fund collaborative. Sponsored by Public Interest Projects, a public charity that incubates social justice projects and collaborative funds, the U.S. Human Rights Fund seeks to expand the base of activists who are integrating international human rights standards and participatory methodologies, such as documentation of abuses and organizing by those directly impacted, into their social justice work.

The Fund has also supported research by The Opportunity Agenda on the relevance of human rights in the domestic U.S. context. The Opportunity Agenda's 2007 study found that, contrary to the assumptions of the Fund's donors and grantees, Americans see human rights as fundamentally relevant to their concerns at home. Eight in 10 polled voters strongly agreed with the statement that "We should strive to uphold human rights in the U.S. because there are people being denied their human rights in our country." Equally unexpected, majorities of polled Americans also said that basic economic and social needs were or should be human rights, such as quality education (82%), access to health care (72%), a living wage (68%), living in a clean environment (68%), and housing (51%).

WHY THE MOVE TO INTEGRATE HUMAN RIGHTS?

Many of those interviewed indicated that the concept of human rights is not a substitute for civil rights or social justice, but an affirmative enhancement of that vision. They see

"Aided by Secretary of State John Foster Dulles, a bloc of southern senators effectively thwarted U.S. implementation of the [Universal Declaration of Human Rights] and subsequent international human rights treaties."

> "Six decades after the creation of the Universal Declaration of Human Rights, there appears to be a return to a more integrated perspective on civil and human rights within the United States."

human rights as a unifying approach that allows them to link previously disintegrated strategies (e.g., litigation, grassroots organizing, and policy work) and multiple issue sectors to one another and connect them to global standards, activism, and enforcement mechanisms. Grantmakers and their grantees pointed to several useful aspects of a human rights approach:

Grassroots Leadership

Virtually all of those interviewed agreed that the new energy around the application of human rights concepts domestically is being fueled largely by the grassroots. Several organizers noted that the idea that all people are born equal in dignity and rights, regardless of citizenship, race, or economic status, is enormously empowering to vulnerable and marginalized people. "Human rights calls for a different process—going to people most affected to ask them what the impact of a law or policy has been," remarked Ramona Ortega, former director of the Human Rights Project and founder of Cidadão Global, a newly formed organization that works with Brazilian immigrants in a local-global context. Veronica Dorsey, a leadership organizer with the United Workers Association (UWA) in Baltimore, MD, said that the human rights framework was fundamental to UWA's successful Living Wages Campaign for day laborers at the Camden Yards stadium. "I was making $7 an hour," said Dorsey, "even though the baseball field sold hot dogs for the same price. I was tired of being treated like a disposable commodity, and the United Workers told me that I didn't have to accept that. I realized that it was about dignity and respect." Ajamu Baraka, director of the U.S. Human Rights Network, talks of a "people-centered human rights movement" and observes that "you can't realize human rights without a shift in the balance of power. People who are directly impacted must drive the process."

Affirmative, Broad Standards

Others said that human rights norms provide a set of positive rights that government is obligated to work incrementally to *fulfill*, alongside U.S. constitutional rights *against* discrimination. "Human rights allow us to articulate a demand for what we really want, as opposed to only talking about what we don't want," said one activist. Human rights legal standards are also often broader and more protective of rights than domestic civil rights statutes. For example, civil rights laws in many areas require a finding of intentional discrimination to trigger a legal remedy. By contrast, the international covenants on race and gender discrimination direct governments to remedy disparate impacts or effects of social policy. Some interviewees noted that the emphasis of human rights on equality of outcomes offers strategic benefits in an era in which discrimination is more often structural, rather than overt.

In particular, several immigrant rights groups, frustrated with a legal trend within the U.S. to limit the rights and benefits of undocumented people and noncitizens, have gravitated to a human rights framework, which articulates basic standards of treatment to which all people are entitled. Karen Narasaki, executive director of the Asian American Justice Center, has been at the forefront of pushing the national traditional civil rights groups to consider incorporating human rights in domestic work. "I have come to believe that there need to be some global standards set on the rights of noncitizens whether they are undocumented or legally present," she said. Narasaki helped to found the Rights Working Group, a coalition that uses human rights framing, forums, and tools alongside traditional civil rights strategies to address the rights of immigrants in the justice system, after 9/11.

A Framework for Addressing Economic Rights

Some of the earliest "second-generation" human rights activists were small anti-poverty groups that organized around economic justice issues like welfare and housing— concerns that the U.S. Constitution does not recognize as rights. By comparison, several human rights treaties that followed the UDHR in the 1960s and 1970s, such as the International Covenant on Economic, Social and Cultural Rights, addressed directly the right to an "adequate standard of living," decent housing, and the "highest attainable standard of health."

Although the United States has never ratified the treaties, some activists nonetheless saw these standards as providing useful organizing principles for their work. The Kensington Welfare Union and the Poor People's Economic Human Rights Campaign, for example, arose in response to Clinton-era welfare reforms and early on adopted a human rights framework for their work. These activists saw themselves picking up the mantle of Martin Luther King Jr.'s unfinished Poor People's Campaign. Indeed, it was Dr. King's growing understanding of what poverty does to human dignity that led him to declare in 1967 that, "It is necessary to realize that we have moved from the era of civil rights to human rights."

Law schools have also begun to explore the application of human rights theories to poverty law practice as well. Two years ago, the Human Rights Institute at Columbia Law School and the Program on Law & the Global Economy at Northeastern University began an initiative to train legal services lawyers to deploy international human rights standards along with more traditional claims in welfare-rights and housing litigation.

But perhaps the most robust use of economic human rights is emerging among immigrant worker organizations, such as the Coalition of Immokalee Workers, the National Network for Immigrant & Refugee Rights, and the National Day Laborers' Organizing Network. These organizations acutely understand modern labor as global phenomena. In a market in which human as well as financial capital flows across borders, they point out that international standards—such as the Convention on the Protection of Rights of All Migrant Workers and their Families—are necessary to guard against exploitation of workers in both sending and receiving nations. For example, the Coalition of Immokalee Workers (CIW), a group of immigrant farm laborers in Florida, uses human rights language, documentation, and participatory organizing in its successful Fair Food Campaign. In the past four years, these largely Spanish-speaking migrant workers have negotiated agreements for higher wages and better working conditions from several corporate food giants. CIW describes human rights as a natural and familiar framework for their members, who come from Mexico, Central America, and Haiti.

The Promise of Commonality and Intersectionality

Several interviewees who worked directly with constituents said that human rights encompassed multiple issues relevant to their communities more readily than civil rights, which is often deployed with a single-identity focus. Jennifer Allen, the director of the Border Action Network in Tucson, AZ, said that her group initially focused on racial profiling at the U.S.–Mexico border through a police brutality lens, and then later an immigrant rights frame. After several years, said Allen, "We made the shift to human rights because [the framework of] immigrant rights didn't help us put our community's struggle in a larger reality. Our folks weren't living and working simply as immigrants—they

"The Opportunity Agenda's 2007 study found that… Americans see human rights as fundamentally relevant to their concerns at home. "

> "The concept of human rights is not a substitute for civil rights or social justice, but an affirmative enhancement of that vision."

also want good education for their kids, a decent place to live, and a better border policy."

Several grantmakers agreed that the human rights framework is a boon to cross-sector thinking and organizing. Alvin Starks, a philanthropic consultant and former program officer at the Arcus Foundation—whose portfolio focused on the intersection of race, gender, and LGBT issues—emphasized the potential of human rights to bridge advocacy silos. "Grantmakers are becoming more open to the human rights analysis, because it allows us to break through our grantmaking silos and establish a more united social justice agenda. I think the human rights analysis has pushed grantmakers to think and redefine how we address the issues that we support." Betsy Brill of Strategic Philanthropy, Ltd. observed that, "Human rights as a tool and a language resonate across race, gender, and other issues. Human rights holds the promise of commonality and the power of intersectionality. It is an umbrella to bring together larger numbers of communities that fundamentally share the basic tenets of human dignity and fairness."

CHALLENGES TO A HUMAN RIGHTS FRAMEWORK

Interest in human rights may be rising, but it is still far from the dominant framework for social justice advocacy. Lawyers in particular were quick to say that the advantages of international human rights law are still more theoretical than practical. Notwithstanding some encouraging citations of international standards by U.S. Supreme Court justices in recent cases—e.g., striking down the execution of the mentally ill (2002), criminal sodomy laws (2003), and the death penalty for juveniles (2005)—human rights treaties still have little traction in domestic courts. Todd Cox, the minority rights program

officer at the Ford Foundation and a former civil rights litigator, observed that "The biggest challenge is in bringing legal challenges in U.S. federal courts. I can litigate a human rights claim in a U.S. court, but there are limitations. At this point, U.S courts are self-contained and do not view themselves as part of a larger global infrastructure."

Another facet of the resistance to human rights, said several grantmakers and grantees, is the historically tense relationship between civil rights activists and human rights activists, who for many years seemed content to ignore racial and gender injustices in their own backyard. This history stretches back some 60 years, to debates between W.E.B. DuBois and Eleanor Roosevelt over how explicitly to address the struggle of black Americans for equal rights in establishing an international system of human rights enforcement.

Today, some activists worry that the universality of the human rights framework diminishes the particular nature of racial and gender injustice. Rinku Sen, executive director of the Applied Research Center, a research and advocacy organization that focuses on structural racism, notes that, "We lead with racial justice so that we can end up with human rights. The reason we don't use human rights alone is that it elides the racial dynamics we're trying to address in the larger society." Sen suggested that the universality of human rights was appealing to some grantmakers and activists who had grown discomfited by a focus on race but opined that "You can't get to human rights without racial justice— how you get to the universal is through the specific."

Sen and others noted that an additional challenge to situating U.S. problems in an international human rights frame was one of relativity—no matter how underenforced our human rights laws may be, they far surpass those of nations that have no rule of law or accountability mechanisms. "To analogize our situation to what is happening in Darfur or Afghanistan is a terrible mistake," said Professor David Dow of the University of Houston Law Center, a lawyer with extensive experience in representing poor and wrongfully convicted defendants in the United States.

Still others suggested that human rights framing was an unnecessary detour to attaining social justice goals. "I understand why people like [the human rights frame] in principle," said Simon Greer, president and CEO of Jewish Funds for Justice. "But on the ground it is not as compelling or resonant as a civil rights or opportunity frame. If you are tapping into American cultural ethos, it's a long way around to educate people about international human rights and its implications. Why not just say, 'What do we expect America to be? We are the land of opportunity; we persist and prevail.' This seems like a much clearer framework that is grounded in our cultural norms and movement history."

LINGERING RESISTANCE AMONG GRANTMAKERS

Most large social justice grantmakers interviewed for this piece viewed human rights framing as an increasing but still marginal trend. "I see human rights emerging at the grassroots, but not so much among the major social justice organizations in my portfolio," noted Geri Mannion of the Carnegie Corporation. Thomasina Williams, program officer for Governance at the Ford Foundation, agreed. "I see it among grantees that are directly engaging with constituents on the ground. But most of my grantees don't talk to us about human rights." Mannion, Williams, and other social justice grantmakers cited several examples of groups whose funding applications never mention human rights.

Yet for the last several years, a number of mainstream social justice organizations have been quietly integrating human rights in their work. For example, the Leadership Conference on Civil Rights formed a human rights task force after the 2001 UN Conference on Racism in Durban, South Africa. LCCR recently issued a report calling for the U.S. Civil Rights Commission to be re-chartered as a "Human and Civil Rights Commission" with an expanded mandate reflecting that change. Legal Momentum, formerly the NOW Legal Defense Fund, has engaged judges in training on human rights. The Center for Reproductive Rights recently drafted a new strategic plan that seeks to integrate human rights, which it had been using in its international program only, throughout all of its work. For the past several years, the Lawyers' Committee for Civil Rights under Law has engaged in international human rights advocacy—filing reports with the United Nations on the United States' failure to comply with international treaties on race and civil rights, and even sending staff to Geneva to lobby United Nations personnel. According to John Brittain, chief counsel and senior deputy director of the Lawyers' Committee, "Our goal is to incorporate international human rights principles in our domestic civil rights work to expand individual rights and remedies. We are trying to incorporate human rights principles in all of our cases, as well as in U.N. advocacy, so that the U.S. Supreme Court will eventually acknowledge them." John Payton, director-counsel of the NAACP Legal Defense & Educational Fund, added that "human rights is the unifying principle in our democracy— it's our history, our present, and how the world wants to see us."

Yet these and other groups say that they hesitate to emphasize human rights in their grant applications for fear that grantmakers will see it as a naïve or underleveraged strategy. In

> "Human rights norms provide a set of positive rights that government is obligated to work incrementally to *fulfill*, alongside U.S. constitutional rights *against* discrimination."

> "Several interviewees...
> said that human rights
> encompassed multiple issues
> relevant to their communities
> more readily than civil rights,
> which is often deployed with a
> single-identity focus."

some foundations, this fear is well founded. More than one grantee described being told to excise the term "human rights" from its proposals. But increasingly, foundations with a history of funding civil rights and social justice are redrafting their guidelines to include human rights. One example is the Overbrook Foundation, which has supported civil rights advocacy since the 1940s. Several years ago, Overbrook created a human rights program, which encourages grantees to explore human rights strategies in their social justice work.

A GENERATIONAL SHIFT?

Several grantmakers and grantees pointed to a generational shift at work across the social justice spectrum. One funder posited that, among older activists and grantmakers, "Some fear that moving beyond civil rights represents a loss of ground." Alan Jenkins of The Opportunity Agenda noted that, "Within the racial justice world, at least, 'civil rights' is not just a word; it's a part of our history and consciousness as African Americans. The human rights strategy is not enough of a reason to relinquish that."

By contrast, Geri Mannion of the Carnegie Corporation remarked that, "Younger people see this as a human rights struggle. They are more international in their context and ask, 'How do our policies on minimum wage and sweatshops compare with practice overseas?' Young people on college campuses get it." Several interviewees observed that these post-baby boomers came of age in an increasingly globalized world of commerce, law, and ideas and tend to be more open to transnational language and the human rights approach than their predecessors.

This increasing fluidity between the international and the domestic is exerting an influence on both grantmakers and social justice organizations. Two younger leaders

in the field—Benjamin Todd Jealous, former executive director of the Rosenberg Foundation and now president and CEO of the NAACP, and Ann Beeson, director of U.S. Programs at the Open Society Institute—spent formative years of their careers at Amnesty International and Human Rights Watch, respectively. Each brought an interest in human rights framing and strategies to their subsequent posts in philanthropy and advocacy. Beeson, for example, helped to convince the National ACLU to create a Human Rights Program, which now litigates human rights claims in U.S. cases on immigrant rights, women's rights, and national security in both domestic courts and international human rights bodies. The program also provides training and technical assistance to help ACLU affiliates around the country integrate human rights strategies.

The emerging human rights movement also includes a substantial number of younger activists who are first-generation immigrants from Latin America and Southeast Asia. Puja Dhawan, a young Indian attorney who grew up in the Middle East and the United States, began her career as a legal services lawyer and later moved to a post at the United Nations. One attraction of her current job, as senior program officer at the U.S. Human Rights Fund, was that it "really allowed me to integrate my identity as an Indian woman with my reality here in the United States."

At the same time, several activists said that the more profound generational shift in the social justice field has been from "civil rights" to "racial justice." Over the past decade, a new wave of advocacy groups, like the Applied Research Center (ARC), the Advancement Project, and the Center for Social Inclusion, has promoted a racial justice framework that focuses on institutional racism and structural exclusion. "Civil rights gave way to anti-racism work in the 1980s, which gave way to a racial justice framework," said Rinku Sen of ARC. In fact, ARC was one of the earliest organizations to make the shift in the 1990s. "If anti-racism was what we're against, then racial justice is what we are for," added Sen. "The shift reflects a desire of activists to have a positive frame, broader than the legal. Racial justice gives you a civic, economic, and cultural frame for the work."

Several advocates and grantmakers cited this same desire for a broader notion of interdependent rights as animating their interest in human rights. Whether advocates refer to their work as social justice, racial justice, or human rights, it is clear that the old divisions between civil and political rights, on one hand, and economic, cultural, and social rights, on the other, are breaking down among a younger generation of activists. These activists see economic and social issues, such as sustainable jobs, quality public education, universal health care, and affordable housing, as the major challenges of our time. They are also seeking to integrate litigation—a preeminent strategy of the civil rights movement—with on-the-ground organizing in affected communities.

Indeed, the integration of human rights into the social justice landscape— rather than opposition to civil rights or social justice—is the operative concept, said Dorothy Thomas, a former program consultant to the U.S. Human Rights Fund and founder of the women's rights program at Human Rights Watch. Thomas notes that the very suggestion that human rights and civil rights are in opposition to one another "suggests that we are hanging on to old ways of thinking. What we might have previously thought of as separate spheres of action, social justice and human rights, are increasingly fundamentally connected and mutually reinforcing. Social justice actors are seeing the value added of human rights, and human rights activists are seeing the necessity of linkage to broader social justice movements."

Thomas does identify one real challenge to integration, however, which is the "mythology" that human rights are merely legal standards, drafted in elite boardrooms in Switzerland and requiring a lawyer to penetrate and courts to enforce. While the normative content of human rights standards provide an enormous asset, "Too often the struggle for human rights gets reduced to a question of treaty ratification, when it is really about…human rights as a vision and a method. We're all born equal in dignity and rights. This notion does not purely reside in the law, but in one's sense of self that can be actualized through direct struggle or through the legal system."

One major opportunity to promote social justice in the United States, she and others point out, is a new recognition among the American public and political leaders that the United States must reclaim allegiance to human rights in its own practices if it is to restore its credibility on the world stage. Catherine Powell, associate professor of law at Fordham University and the author of *Human Rights at Home: A Domestic Policy Blueprint for the New Administration,* suggests that closing the Guantánamo Bay detention center and renouncing torture are important, but alone inadequate, steps in a larger agenda on domestic human rights. An effective agenda must also include addressing a growing gap between rich and poor in the United States, 45 million citizens without basic health care, and the highest incarceration rate of any country in the world. Reclaiming human rights as a fundamentally American concept is an idea whose time has come, said Harold Honghu Koh, dean of the Yale Law School and a former senior State Department official, at a recent event at the Center for American Progress focused on domestic human rights. Koh remarked that "Apple pie, which as I recall was invented in Bavaria, would be lucky to be as American as human rights."

"Another facet of the resistance to human rights… is the historically tense relationship between civil rights activists and human rights activists, who for many years seemed content to ignore racial and gender injustices in their own backyard."

> "The United States must reclaim allegiance to human rights in its own practices if it is to restore its credibility on the world stage."

Indeed, the idea of an inalienable human right to dignity and freedom is at the heart of the American identity. It animates our Declaration of Independence and runs through our struggles against slavery, for women's suffrage, and for civil rights. "Where, after all, do universal human rights begin?" asked Eleanor Roosevelt famously. "In small places, close to home."

ENDNOTE

1. Tanya Coke is a consultant to foundations and social justice nonprofits, and former Program Manager for the U.S. Human Rights Fund.

4 Trends in Social Justice Grantmaking

By Sherry Seward

Social justice grantmaking is represented in all areas of foundation activity, from education to health to the environment. This chapter documents the dimensions of social justice giving based on a sample of the largest U.S. independent, corporate, community, and operating foundations in 2006, and changes in funding priorities since 2002. It seeks to answer questions such as: Did social justice funding keep pace with overall growth in foundation giving during this period? How did giving priorities change? Which grantmakers accounted for the largest shares of social justice grantmaking?

CHANGES IN SOCIAL JUSTICE GIVING, 2002 TO 2006

* Social justice funding grew faster than overall giving between 2002 and 2006

* Giving for social justice-related activities reached $2.3 billion in 2006

* Bill & Melinda Gates Foundation accounted for over half of growth in grant dollars

Providing support for domestic and international social justice activities continues to be an important priority for a number of U.S. foundations. Overall, giving for social justice-related purposes by sampled foundations rose nearly 31 percent between 2002 and 2006, surpassing the roughly 20 percent increase in foundation giving overall (Figure 4-1). Actual grant dollars totaled $2.3 billion in the latest year, up from roughly

$1.8 billion in 2002 (Table 4-1).[1] As a result, social justice-related funding accounted for 12 percent of overall grant dollars in 2006, compared to 11 percent in 2002. The number of social justice grants awarded also rose at a faster-than-average pace— 14.6 percent versus 10 percent—and totaled 15,302 in the latter year.

The relatively more rapid growth of social justice-related giving during the latest period contrasted with the 1998 to 2002 period, when this type of funding grew more slowly. Moreover, Figure 4-2 and Table 4-2 show that social justice funding in 2006 not only surpassed the share of overall grant dollars in 2002, but also slightly exceeded the share recorded in 1998. By comparison, the social justice field has benefited from steady, albeit modest growth in the share of number of grants it represents.

Numerous factors contributed to the increase in social justice-related

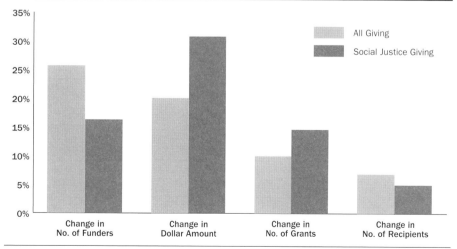

| FIGURE 4-1 | Change in Social Justice Giving vs. All Giving, 2002 and 2006 |

Source: The Foundation Center, *Social Justice Grantmaking II*, 2009. Based on all grants of $10,000 or more awarded by a sample of 1,005 larger foundations for 2002 and 1,263 for 2006.

grantmaking during this period, from a return to growth in overall foundation giving following the early 2000s economic downturn to the accession of the nation's largest grantmaker—the Bill & Melinda Gates Foundation—into the role of the country's top social justice funder. Between 2002 and 2006, the Gates Foundation's social justice-related giving jumped from $59.1 million to $355.1 million. This increased support accounted for well over half of the more than $541 million rise in social justice-related giving during this period.

This finding might suggest that the Gates Foundation was the primary force driving the growth in social justice grantmaking. However, excluding the Gates Foundation from both the 2002 and 2006 grants sample, social justice funding would *still* have risen more quickly than overall foundation giving during this period (14.4 percent versus 11.3 percent).

Among sampled foundations, 871 funders made at least one social justice-related grant in 2006, up from 749 funders in 2002. However, the sample also increased in size during this period, and the percentage of foundations making social justice grants slipped from 74.5 percent in 2002 to 69 percent. This finding in part reflects the fact that larger foundations in the sample were more likely to make social justice-related grants than were the relatively smaller foundations that have been added since 2002.

Compared to the increases in social justice dollars and number of grants, the number of organizations receiving

TABLE 4-1 Change in Social Justice Giving, 1998 to 2006

Year	No. of Funders	% Change	Grant Dollars	% Change	No. of Grants	% Change	No. of Recipients	% Change
1998	686		$1,148,846		9,975		5,071	
2002	749	9.2	1,759,536	53.4	13,355	33.9	6,625	30.6
2006	871	16.3	2,300,763	30.8	15,302	14.6	6,955	5.0

Source: The Foundation Center, *Social Justice Grantmaking II*, 2009. Dollar figures in thousands. Based on all grants of $10,000 or more awarded by a sample of more than 1,000 larger foundations.

FIGURE 4-2 Social Justice Giving as a Share of All Giving, 2002 and 2006

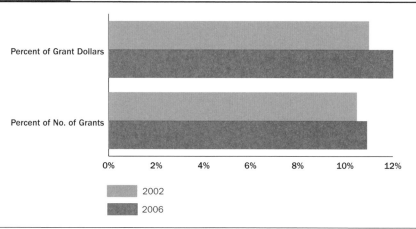

Source: The Foundation Center, *Social Justice Grantmaking II*, 2009. Based on all grants of $10,000 or more awarded by a sample of 1,005 larger foundations for 2002 and 1,263 for 2006.

TABLE 4-2 Social Justice Giving as a Percentage of All Giving, 1998 to 2006

Year	No. of Social Justice Funders	No. of All Funders	%	Social Justice Grant Dollars	All Grant Dollars	%	No. of Social Justice Grants	No. of All Grants	%	No. of Social Justice Recipients	No. of All Recipients	%
1998	686	1,009	68.0	$1,148,846	$9,711,394	11.8	9,975	97,220	10.3	5,071	40,934	12.4
2002	749	1,005	74.5	1,759,536	15,924,894	11.0	13,355	127,728	10.5	6,625	52,375	12.6
2006	871	1,263	69.0	2,300,763	19,123,032	12.0	15,302	140,484	10.9	6,955	56,015	12.4

Source: The Foundation Center, *Social Justice Grantmaking II*, 2009. Dollar figures in thousands. Based on all grants of $10,000 or more awarded by a sample of 1,009 larger foundations for 1998, 1,005 for 2002, and 1,263 for 2006.

support grew at a slower pace. The number of recipients of social justice funding grew 5 percent, from 6,625 organizations in 2002 to 6,955 organizations in 2006. This compares to nearly 7 percent growth in the overall number of recipients in the sample and may reflect a narrower pool of nonprofit organizations that engage in social justice-related work.

SOCIAL JUSTICE GIVING BY FOUNDATION TYPE AND PERIOD OF ESTABLISHMENT

Foundation characteristics can often have a pronounced impact on giving priorities. To provide perspective on the impact of these differences on social justice grantmaking, the following analysis examines giving trends based on foundation type (independent, corporate, and community) and period of establishment (before 1950, 1950 through 1969, 1970 through 1989, and 1990 to present).

Social Justice Giving by Foundation Type

* Independent and family foundations provided the vast majority of social justice grant dollars and grants in 2006

* Corporate foundations accounted for roughly one-fifth of funders and grants

Consistent with 2002, independent foundations—including family foundations—provided the vast majority of social justice funding in the latest year. Figure 4-3 shows that these foundations accounted for 84.4 percent of social justice grant dollars and close to two-thirds (62.4 percent) of the number of grants. In fact, 21 of the top 25 social justice grantmakers in the latest year were independents, up from 18 funders in 2002. Still, as a group, independent foundations saw slight decreases in their shares of funders, grants dollars, and grants between 2002 and 2006.

Compared to independent foundations, corporate foundations provided a modest 8.8 percent of social justice-related grant dollars in 2006. However, they accounted for nearly one-fifth (19.1 percent) of social justice funders and over one-fifth (22.9 percent) of the grants awarded in the social justice sample. The differences in shares of grant dollars and number of grants reflects corporate foundations' tendency to award a greater number of relatively smaller grants, which primarily support economic, housing, and educational opportunities for disadvantaged minorities and other groups within the

areas in which they operate. Corporate foundations also slightly increased their shares of grant dollars and grants in the latest period. Two corporate foundations ranked among the top 25 social justice funders in 2006—the Bank of America and Citi foundations.

Giving by community foundations for social justice-related activities totaled just over 5 percent of grant dollars but almost 13 percent of grants. These shares were up from 2002. Similar to corporate foundations, community foundations tend to provide a greater number of relatively smaller grants. In 2006, the Peninsula Community

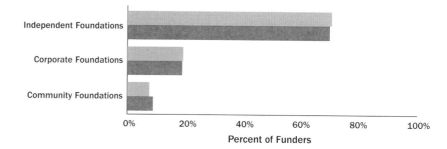

FIGURE 4-3 Distribution of Social Justice Funders by Foundation Type, 2002 and 2006

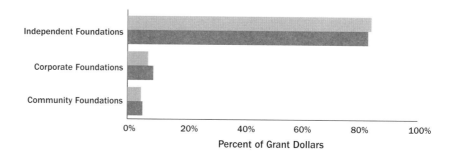

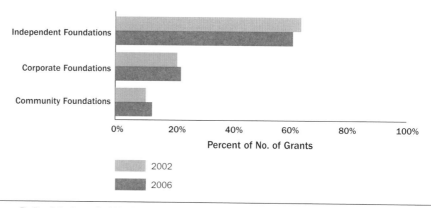

Source: The Foundation Center, *Social Justice Grantmaking II*, 2009. Based on all grants of $10,000 or more awarded by a sample of 749 larger foundations for 2002 and 871 for 2006. Excludes giving by operating foundations.

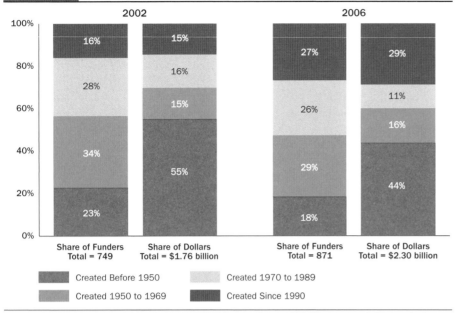

FIGURE 4-4 | Distribution of Social Justice Funders by Period of Establishment, 2002 and 2006

Source: The Foundation Center, *Social Justice Grantmaking II*, 2009. Based on all grants of $10,000 or more awarded by a sample of 749 larger foundations for 2002 and 871 for 2006. Due to rounding, figures may not total 100 percent.

Foundation[2] was the only community foundation represented among the top 25 social justice funders. In contrast, two other community foundations ranked among the top 25 social justice grantmakers in 2002— the New York Community Trust and San Diego Foundation.

Social Justice Giving by Period of Establishment

◆ **Foundations established before 1950 provided the largest share of social justice support in 2006**

◆ **Social justice funders established since 1990 doubled their share of giving between 2002 and 2006**

As a group, grantmakers established before 1950 commanded the largest share of social justice funding

TABLE 4-3 | 25 Largest Social Justice Funders, 2006

'02 Rank	'06 Rank	Foundation Name	State	Type*	Amount	%	No. of Grants	%	% Change in Social Justice Giving, '02 to '06	Social Justice Giving as a % of the Foundation's Giving
6.	1.	Bill & Melinda Gates Foundation	WA	IN	$355,092,312	15.4	90	0.6	500.4	14.1
1.	2.	Ford Foundation	NY	IN	281,192,706	12.2	1,007	6.6	-0.1	53.2
4.	3.	W.K. Kellogg Foundation	MI	IN	142,576,124	6.2	281	1.8	99.4	50.1
5.	4.	Rockefeller Foundation	NY	IN	92,954,262	4.0	98	0.6	56.4	66.7
3.	5.	John D. and Catherine T. MacArthur Foundation	IL	IN	83,137,012	3.6	218	1.4	10.1	45.1
2.	6.	Robert Wood Johnson Foundation	NJ	IN	73,686,008	3.2	164	1.1	-49.3	20.9
7.	7.	California Endowment	CA	IN	61,996,613	2.7	254	1.7	10.8	50.9
9.	8.	Annie E. Casey Foundation	MD	IN	59,491,179	2.6	562	3.7	23.7	57.6
14.	9.	William and Flora Hewlett Foundation	CA	IN	41,989,100	1.8	116	0.8	58.3	15.3
8.	10.	Charles Stewart Mott Foundation	MI	IN	33,591,069	1.5	234	1.5	-30.9	33.8
24.	11.	Northwest Area Foundation	MN	IN	31,499,589	1.4	39	0.3	148.2	77.6
12.	12.	Open Society Institute	NY	OP	31,180,450	1.4	237	1.5	-3.1	45.8
13.	13.	Carnegie Corporation of New York	NY	IN	27,572,900	1.2	140	0.9	-6.4	36.4
23.	14.	Citi Foundation	NY	CS	23,107,935	1.0	354	2.3	68.8	27.1
–	15.	Marguerite Casey Foundation	WA	IN	21,585,163	0.9	139	0.9	N/A	79.7
54.	16.	Bank of America Charitable Foundation	NC	CS	20,299,981	0.9	306	2.0	371.9	20.6
37.	17.	Susan Thompson Buffett Foundation	NE	IN	19,641,506	0.9	19	0.1	188.3	19.6
60.	18.	Starr Foundation	NY	IN	18,859,314	0.8	23	0.2	379.9	4.6
31.	19.	California Wellness Foundation	CA	IN	18,223,000	0.8	88	0.6	92.8	36.7
38.	20.	Joyce Foundation	IL	IN	15,092,555	0.7	48	0.3	132.2	31.3
96.	21.	Evelyn and Walter Haas, Jr. Fund	CA	IN	15,071,250	0.7	176	1.2	575.8	57.2
–	22.	JEHT Foundation[1]	NY	IN	14,630,743	0.6	116	0.8	N/A	58.8
93.	23.	Peninsula Community Foundation	CA	CM	14,606,402	0.6	105	0.7	518.6	18.1
40.	24.	John S. and James L. Knight Foundation	FL	IN	14,076,000	0.6	18	0.1	122.4	19.7
16.	25.	James Irvine Foundation	CA	IN	13,426,500	0.6	61	0.4	-39.3	20.6
		Subtotal			**$1,524,579,673**	**66.3**	**4,893**	**32.0**		
		All Other Foundations			776,183,010	33.7	10,410	68.0		
		Total			$2,300,762,683	100.0	15,302	100.0		

Source: Source: The Foundation Center, *Social Justice Grantmaking II*, 2009. Based on all grants of $10,000 or more awarded by a sample of 749 larger foundations for 2002 and 871 for 2006. Due to rounding, some figures may not total 100 percent.
*IN=Independent; CS=Corporate; CM=Community; OP=Operating
[1]The foundation ceased operation in Jaunary 2009.
– = Not included in the 2002 social justice grantmaking set.
N/A = Not available.

in 2006, accounting for nearly 44 percent of grant dollars (Figure 4-4). In fact, five of these grantmakers awarded $50 million or more for social justice in the latest year—the Ford Foundation ($281.2 million), W.K. Kellogg Foundation ($142.6 million), Rockefeller Foundation ($93 million), Robert Wood Johnson Foundation ($73.7 million), and Annie E. Casey Foundation ($59.5 million).

During the same time period, social justice giving by more recently established foundations grew considerably. In fact, foundations established since 1990 accounted for almost 29 percent of social justice giving in 2006, double their share in 2002 and significantly more than grantmakers established in the 1950s and 1960s (16.3 percent) and the 1970s and 1980s (11.2 percent).

The number of social justice grantmakers established after 1989 also grew substantially—from a 16 percent share of funders in 2002 to a roughly 27 percent share in 2006. Of the 233 social justice funders established since 1990, the top three by giving were the Bill & Melinda Gates Foundation (1994), California Endowment (1996), and Open Society Institute (1993). Among funders established more recently were the Paul Allen Family Foundation (2005), Omidyar Network Fund (2004), and Robert W. Wilson Charitable Trust (2003).

Led by the William and Flora Hewlett Foundation (1966), foundations established in the 1950s and 1960s provided just over 16 percent of social justice dollars and represented a 29 percent share of the funders. Other large grantmakers in this group included the Susan Thompson Buffett Foundation (1964), which has benefited from Warren Buffett's recent historic commitment to philanthropy as well as a bequest from the estate of Susan Buffett, and Bank of America Charitable Foundation (1958). By comparison, grantmakers established in the 1970s and 1980s commanded the smallest share of giving (11.2 percent) among the groups. However, the share of current social justice funders in the sample that were established during this time period (25.8 percent) was similar to those established since 1990 (26.8 percent). By far, the leading social justice funder established in the 1970s or 1980s was the John D. and Catherine T. MacArthur Foundation (1970).

TRENDS AMONG LEADING SOCIAL JUSTICE FUNDERS

- Top 25 social justice funders provided over two-thirds of grant dollars in 2006

- Funding by Gates, Ford, and Kellogg foundations accounted for more than one-third of overall support

The 25 largest social justice funders in the United States have a significant impact on grantmaking trends in the field. These foundations provided $1.5 billion of the $2.3 billion awarded by all social justice funders in 2006. Among the 871 foundations in the sample, the 25 largest social justice givers accounted for two-thirds (66.3 percent) of giving (Table 4-3). However, this share was down slightly from 2002 (67.7 percent).

THE IMPACT OF THE ECONOMIC CRISIS ON SOCIAL JUSTICE GRANTMAKING

Social justice-related giving by U.S. foundations continued to grow in 2007. Funding for social justice by grantmakers included in the Foundation Center's grants sample reached $3 billion, or 13.7 percent of overall grant dollars that year. (The share of number of grants remained almost unchanged at 10.7 percent.) Nonetheless, the outlook for social justice grantmaking, and foundation giving overall, changed dramatically as a result of the economic crisis that took hold in 2008.

In the midst of a deepening economic downturn, the Foundation Center has estimated that the nation's grantmaking foundations increased their giving 2.8 percent in 2008. Although this change amounted to a 1 percent decrease after inflation, foundation giving nonetheless remained remarkably stable given the severity of the downturn. Looking ahead, however, the Center expects that foundation giving will decrease in the range of the high single digits to low double digits in 2009 and decline further in 2010.[1]

What does this mean for social justice-related funding? Undoubtedly, grant dollars for social justice will decrease in the near term, as they will for all areas of activity. But there is no reason to expect that social justice-related grantmaking will be disproportionately affected by the crisis.

Supporting this conclusion are findings from a Foundation Center research advisory, which showed that the economic downturn of the early 2000s did not have a discernable impact on foundations' funding priorities.[2] Findings from an early 2009 survey buttress this conclusion, with the vast majority of foundation respondents reporting that they do not anticipate changing the number of program areas they currently support.[3] Moreover, given the recent change in administration in the United States and the impact of the economic crisis on already disadvantaged populations, there may be even greater incentive for foundations to seek out opportunities to support social justice.

Endnotes

1. See Lawrence, S., and R. Mukai, *Foundation Growth and Giving Estimates: Current Outlook,* New York: Foundation Center, 2009.
2. See Lawrence, S., *Do Foundation Giving Priorities Change in Times of Economic Distress?,* New York: Foundation Center, 2008.
3. See Lawrence, S., *Foundations Address the Impact of the Economic Crisis,* New York: Foundation Center, 2009.

Together, the three largest funders—the Bill & Melinda Gates Foundation (WA), Ford Foundation (NY), and W.K. Kellogg Foundation (MI)—provided over one-third of total social justice support. Nonetheless, this tremendous concentration of resources among the largest funders is not unusual. For example, the top 25 international funders in 2006 represented 79 percent of overall international giving.

Giving by the top 25 funders grew by $332.6 million between 2002 and 2006. This almost 28 percent growth was surpassed by the close to 31 percent increase in overall social justice giving. The number of grants awarded by the top social justice funders also grew more slowly—2.3 percent versus 14.6 percent.

TABLE 4-4 | 50 Largest Funders by Share of Giving for Social Justice, 2006

Foundation Name	State	Social Justice Grants	Social Justice Giving as a % of the Foundation's Giving	No. of Social Justice Grants
1. Rosenberg Foundation	CA	$3,512,000	97.3	34
2. Marguerite Casey Foundation	WA	21,585,163	79.7	139
3. Moriah Fund	DC	6,788,254	79.5	187
4. A Glimmer of Hope Foundation	TX	4,531,837	77.7	1
5. Northwest Area Foundation	MN	31,499,589	77.6	39
6. Jessie Smith Noyes Foundation	NY	2,868,000	75.6	61
7. WellPoint Foundation	CA	10,653,800	71.0	11
8. Melville Charitable Trust	MA	4,281,736	69.0	18
9. Rockefeller Foundation	NY	92,954,262	66.7	98
10. Mertz Gilmore Foundation	NY	2,233,100	62.0	32
11. JEHT Foundation[1]	NY	14,630,743	58.8	116
12. Robert Sterling Clark Foundation	NY	2,968,885	58.7	38
13. Smith Richardson Foundation	CT	8,525,807	57.6	71
14. New York Foundation	NY	2,347,000	57.6	54
15. Annie E. Casey Foundation	MD	59,491,179	57.6	562
16. Gill Foundation	CO	5,380,791	57.5	131
17. Evelyn and Walter Haas, Jr. Fund	CA	15,071,250	57.2	176
18. Fannie Mae Foundation	DC	8,750,000	56.1	106
19. Public Welfare Foundation	DC	10,478,000	56.0	183
20. Ford Foundation	NY	281,192,706	53.2	1,007
21. California Endowment	CA	61,996,613	50.9	254
22. F. B. Heron Foundation	NY	5,260,000	50.2	52
23. W.K. Kellogg Foundation	MI	142,576,124	50.1	281
24. California Community Foundation	CA	5,072,383	48.2	16
25. Wallace Global Fund	DC	3,583,500	46.9	66
26. Josiah Macy, Jr. Foundation	NY	$2,230,487	46.1	4
27. Open Society Institute	NY	31,180,450	45.8	237
28. John D. and Catherine T. MacArthur Foundation	IL	83,137,012	45.1	218
29. Z. Smith Reynolds Foundation	NC	7,311,000	44.4	86
30. Union Bank of California Foundation	CA	1,365,000	44.3	52
31. Ted Arison Charitable Trust	FL	3,750,000	41.6	1
32. Fund for New Jersey	NJ	1,350,000	41.5	21
33. Compton Foundation	CA	2,205,478	40.7	55
34. Wachovia Regional Foundation	PA	1,943,000	40.7	42
35. Wallace Alexander Gerbode Foundation	CA	1,182,000	40.6	51
36. Alan B. Slifka Foundation	NY	1,870,000	39.1	25
37. Case Foundation	DC	1,490,185	38.4	7
38. Commonwealth Fund	NY	5,844,225	38.1	38
39. S. H. Cowell Foundation	CA	2,511,500	37.3	21
40. John Merck Fund	MA	4,690,750	36.8	67
41. California Wellness Foundation	CA	18,223,000	36.7	88
42. Carnegie Corporation of New York	NY	27,572,900	36.4	140
43. Charles Stewart Mott Foundation	MI	33,591,069	33.8	234
44. The Overbrook Foundation	NY	2,413,500	33.4	56
45. Otto Bremer Foundation	MN	7,922,576	33.0	207
46. Ochylski Family Foundation	IA	1,050,000	32.3	4
47. Banyan Tree Foundation	DC	1,452,716	32.3	20
48. Levi Strauss Foundation	CA	2,215,342	31.8	54
49. The Joyce Foundation	IL	15,092,555	31.3	48
50. Travelers Foundation	MN	2,230,500	31.2	60

Source: The Foundation Center, *Social Justice Grantmaking II*, 2009. Based on all grants of $10,000 or more awarded by a sample of 871 larger foundations. Includes only foundations that provided at least $1 million for social justice-related purposes.
[1]The Foundation ceased operation in January 2009.

Despite notable shifts among the ranks of the top social justice funders, nine funders were included in the top 10 in both 2002 and 2006. In the latter year, the Bill & Melinda Gates Foundation replaced the Ford Foundation as the funder awarding the most social justice dollars, but the Ford Foundation continued to award by far the largest number of social justice grants. New to the top 10 was the ninth-ranked William and Flora Hewlett Foundation (CA), which rose from 14th in 2002. Hewlett replaced the McKnight Foundation (MN), which dropped from the list of top 25 social justice funders. Among social justice funders ranked 16th to 25th, 10 were new to the list.

Examples of funders that substantially raised their level of social justice giving or joined the top 25 group in 2006 include the:

◆ **Bill & Melinda Gates Foundation**, established in 1994 and now the largest foundation in the United States. The foundation also became the top social justice funder in 2006, after increasing its social justice giving by more than 500 percent—from $59.1 million in 2002 to $355.1 million in 2006. This $296 million increase accounted for more than half of the overall gain in social justice grant dollars in the latest period. The vast majority of the foundation's giving supported economic and community development—primarily to establish a new "Green Revolution" in Africa in partnership with the Rockefeller Foundation—followed by health care access and affordability.

◆ **Rockefeller Foundation**, which rose in rank from fifth to fourth after increasing its social justice-related giving by $33.5 million between 2002 and 2006. The foundation awarded the largest social justice-related grant in the latest sample—$50 million to the Nairobi-based Alliance for a Green Revolution in Africa to help bring

the "Green Revolution" to the continent.[3] (See "Economic and Community Development" for further details.)

◆ **Marguerite Casey Foundation,**[4] established in 2001 and ranked 15th with $21.6 million in social justice grants. Dedicated to creating a movement of working families advocating on their own behalf for change, the foundation's largest social justice-related grant in the latest year was a $1.5 million award to the Association of Community Organizations for Reform Now (ACORN) to continue and expand its community mobilization work in the West, Midwest, and Deep South regions.

◆ **Bank of America Charitable Foundation**, one of only two company-sponsored foundations included among the top 25 social justice funders. The foundation jumped in rank from 54th in 2002 to 16th in the latest year, and its four largest grants focused on housing and community development.

◆ **Susan Thompson Buffett Foundation**, which was new to the top 25 funders with $19.6 million in social justice-related giving. Named for the wife of investor Warren Buffett, the foundation has benefited from a bequest from the estate of Susan Buffett and a pledge worth approximately $3 billion from Mr. Buffett to be put into the foundation

over time. The foundation maintains a significant focus on reproductive health care and rights.

◆ **Evelyn and Walter Haas, Jr. Fund**, which jumped in rank from 96th in 2002 to 21st in 2006. The Fund's social justice-related giving increased close to sevenfold during that time period to reach $15.1 million. Haas' grantmaking focuses on helping to ensure that disadvantaged and vulnerable groups—including immigrants, gays and lesbians, people of color, and children—are able to achieve their full potential.

◆ **Peninsula Community Foundation**, which was the only community foundation included among the top 25 social justice funders. Its giving grew by more than 500 percent to reach $14.6 million in 2006. Much of its social justice-related funding in 2006 focused on combating genocide and human trafficking, including a $2.6 million grant to the DC-based Center for American Progress to build an advocacy movement focused on the need to better respond to and ultimately end mass atrocities, and in particular, bring an end to the genocide in Sudan.

Other top 25 foundations reporting at least a near doubling in their social justice grantmaking between 2002 and 2006 included the W.K. Kellogg, Northwest Area, Starr, Joyce, and John S. and James L. Knight foundations. In contrast, five of the 25 largest social

| TABLE 4-5 | Social Justice Grants by Grant Size, 2006 |

Grants Range	No. of Grants	%	Amount	%
$10 million and over	18	0.1	$330,261	14.4
$5 million–under $10 million	22	0.1	136,785	5.9
$1 million–under $5 million	263	1.7	476,018	20.7
$500,000–under $1 million	398	2.6	255,497	11.1
$100,000–under $500,000	3,922	25.6	754,716	32.8
$50,000–under $100,000	2,941	19.2	182,245	7.9
$25,000–under $50,000	3,359	22.0	103,722	4.5
$10,000–under $25,000	4,379	28.6	61,515	2.7
Total	15,302	100.0	$2,300,763	100.0

Source: The Foundation Center, *Social Justice Grantmaking II*, 2009. Dollar figures in thousands. Based on all grants of $10,000 or more awarded by a sample of 871 larger foundations.

TABLE 4-6 | 25 Largest Social Justice Grants

	Recipient	Recipient State/Country	Foundation	Foundation State	Amount	Purpose
1.	Alliance for a Green Revolution in Africa	Kenya	Rockefeller Foundation	NY	$50,000,000	Toward improving productivity and profitability of small-scale farming in Africa through Program for Africa's Seed Systems
2.	United Nations Foundation	DC	Bill & Melinda Gates Foundation	WA	29,911,740	To help crop breeders in Africa to develop improved crop varieties for food security and poverty alleviation
3.	Alliance for a Green Revolution in Africa	Kenya	Bill & Melinda Gates Foundation	WA	28,667,000	To increase African food security by funding network of crop breeders to improve African crop varieties
4.	Bangladesh Rural Advance Commission (BRAC)	Bangladesh	Bill & Melinda Gates Foundation	WA	25,200,929	To demonstrate effective and transferable program model for improving maternal, newborn, and child health in poor urban communities of developing countries
5.	Alliance for a Green Revolution in Africa	Kenya	Bill & Melinda Gates Foundation	WA	24,667,000	To improve access of poor farmers to agricultural technologies in Africa
6.	International Bank for Reconstruction and Development	DC	Bill & Melinda Gates Foundation	WA	23,885,167	To increase access to financial services for the poor by testing and promoting use of innovative information and communication technologies (CGAP)
7.	Alliance for a Green Revolution in Africa	Kenya	Bill & Melinda Gates Foundation	WA	17,333,000	To provide operational support grant to Program for Africa's Seed Systems
8.	Alliance for a Green Revolution in Africa	Kenya	Bill & Melinda Gates Foundation	WA	16,000,000	To increase access of smallholder farmers to improved crop varieties using a variety of production and distribution strategies
9.	Bangladesh Rural Advance Commission (BRAC)	Bangladesh	Bill & Melinda Gates Foundation	WA	14,967,043	To implement integrated microfinance, agriculture, and health programs aimed at the poorest segments of the rural population in Tanzania
10.	International Development Enterprises	CO	Bill & Melinda Gates Foundation	WA	13,444,609	To develop small-plot water technologies, technology markets, and connect farmers to fruit and vegetable markets in Ethiopia, Zambia, Nepal, and Myanmar
11.	Alliance for a Green Revolution in Africa	Kenya	Bill & Melinda Gates Foundation	WA	13,333,000	For increased numbers of African agriculturalists trained in practical methods of breeding and seed systems development
12.	Asian Vegetable Research and Development Center	Sub-Saharan Africa; Mali	Bill & Melinda Gates Foundation	WA	12,083,990	To increase the vegetable production, marketing, and consumption and foster rural development to improve the health of vulnerable groups, in particular poor women and children in sub-Saharan Africa
13.	ActionAid USA	DC	Bill & Melinda Gates Foundation	WA	10,741,823	To develop the capacity of NGOs working within Europe to increase interest and support of governments and institutions in achieving global health Millennium Development Goals
14.	United Nations High Commissioner for Refugees	Switzerland	Bill & Melinda Gates Foundation	WA	10,025,875	To facilitate safe repatriation of Sudanese refugees
15.	Carnegie Endowment for International Peace	DC	William and Flora Hewlett Foundation	CA	10,000,000	For general support of CEIP's New Vision Initiative
16.	California, State of	CA	WellPoint Foundation	CA	10,000,000	For outreach to uninsured
17.	Center for Global Development	DC	Bill & Melinda Gates Foundation	WA	10,000,000	To amplify impact of CGD's policy research and outreach on key public policy debates affecting health, education, governance, and economic outcomes in developing world
18.	Turtle Mountain Band of Chippewa Indians	ND	Northwest Area Foundation	MN	10,000,000	For Pathways to Prosperity Poverty Reduction Strategies, a plan which focuses on mobilizing reservation for poverty reduction, youth leadership, making full use of income supplements, establishing Enterprise Center to spur business ownership and jobs, revitalization of downtown Belcourt, and using tax credits to develop housing, utilities, and economic engines of tourism
19.	Cheyenne River Sioux Tribe	SD	Northwest Area Foundation	MN	9,500,000	For Ventures Poverty Reduction Plan to support a strategic plan which focuses on workforce and economic development, promoting income-generating opportunities in remote settlements, youth leadership internships, improving cross-reservation communications, establishing financial literacy and individual savings account programs
20.	University of New Mexico Foundation	NM	Robert Wood Johnson Foundation	NJ	8,000,000	For endowment for the Robert Wood Johnson Foundation Center for Health Policy. The Center will contribute to development and implementation of national health policies by increasing the number of Hispanic and Native American scholars who can engage in health care policy debate as leaders
21.	Big Thought	TX	Wallace Foundation	NY	8,000,000	For the Dallas Arts Learning Initiative, which will raise the quality of and access to arts learning for all Dallas youth in and out of school by coordinating and strengthening providers, communicating opportunities, and reducing barriers
22.	Joint Center for Political and Economic Studies	DC	W.K. Kellogg Foundation	MI	7,350,000	To reduce health disparities by mobilizing leadership in 20 communities and select national partners
23.	International Rescue Committee	NY	Starr Foundation	NY	7,000,000	To endow Freedom Fund
24.	Nuclear Threat Initiative	DC	Susan Thompson Buffett Foundation	NE	7,000,000	For general support
25.	Council of Michigan Foundations	MI	W.K. Kellogg Foundation	MI	6,500,000	To ensure that Michigan Early Childhood Investment Corporation has the leadership, organizational, and financial capacity necessary to serve as a focal point for early childhood system building; formalize operating agreements with intermediate school districts; and provide local technical assistance that results in every child entering school healthy and ready to learn

Source: The Foundation Center, *Social Justice Grantmaking II*, 2009. Based on all grants of $10,000 or more awarded by a sample of 871 larger foundations.
Note: Grant descriptions have been abbreviated.

justice funders reduced their giving during this period: the Robert Wood Johnson Foundation (down 49.3 percent), James Irvine Foundation (down 39.3 percent), Charles Stewart Mott Foundation (down 30.9 percent), Carnegie Corporation of New York (down 6.4 percent), and Open Society Institute (down 3.1 percent). Finally, the Ford Foundation's giving remained virtually unchanged during this period.

The largest funders also showed a strong commitment to social justice-related activities as measured by the percentage of giving they allocated to this area. Among the top 25 social justice funders in 2006, nine provided at least half of their overall giving for social justice-related activities, while an additional five provided at least one-third. By comparison, in 2002 only three top funders allocated half or more of their giving for social justice-related activities, and 10 provided at least one-third.

Among all 871 social justice funders included in the latest sample, about one-quarter (222) allocated at least 10 percent of their support for social justice-related activities, 52 foundations (6 percent) provided at least one-third, and just 25 foundations (3 percent) allocated at least half of their grant dollars for social justice purposes (Table 4-4).

SOCIAL JUSTICE GRANTS BY GRANT SIZE

- Half of social justice grants were for less than $50,000 in 2006
- The number of very large awards has more than doubled since 2002

Table 4-5 shows that slightly over half of all social justice grants totaled between $10,000 and $49,999 in 2006—comparable to the share reported for 2002. On the other end

of the giving spectrum, the number of very large grants—those of $5 million or more—doubled over the same time period, from 19 grants in 2002 to 40 grants in 2006. These large grants accounted for more than 20 percent of all social justice giving in the latest sample, up from 14.1 percent in 2002. (See Table 4-6 for a list of the 25 largest social justice grants in 2006.)

Consistent with the increase in the number of large awards, the mean or average social justice grant grew by 14.1 percent, from $131,751 in 2002 to $150,357 in 2006. However, an examination of changes in the median grant amount, which is not skewed by the largest grants, showed a much smaller increase. The median social justice grant grew 3.4 percent during this period, from $43,500 to $45,000. (See Table 4-8 for comparisons of average and median grant amounts by subject areas.)

PUBLIC POLICY-RELATED SOCIAL JUSTICE GRANTMAKING

- **Over one-quarter of social justice giving explicitly supported public policy research and reform**

Foundations may take a variety of approaches to secure an equitable distribution of resources and rights in society, from funding the construction of low-income housing to ensuring access to health care for immigrant populations. Supporting efforts to inform the policymaking process at the national or local level across a range of issue areas represents one important component of this work. In 2006, sampled grantmakers specifically directed close to 28 percent of their social justice dollars ($634.1 million) and over 15 percent of their grants (2,354) for public policy research or reform.

While all social justice fields benefited from public policy-related giving, fully half of this support targeted two areas: efforts to foster economic opportunity and community development for vulnerable populations ($186.9 million); and efforts to increase access to and the affordability of health

care ($131.8 million). Among these grants, the California Endowment awarded $192,000 to the California Black Health Network for its Health Policy Advocacy for African Americans program. Other social justice fields receiving at least 5 percent of policy-related dollars included educational reform and access, human services, human rights and civil liberties, and international affairs, peace, and conflict resolution.

Beyond this support, social justice-related grantmaking that does not specifically target public policy research and reform may nonetheless contribute to policy change. For example, a grant supporting research on the disenfranchisement of disadvantaged populations during prior elections may ultimately help to inform government discussions on election reform. Arguably, most social justice funding aimed at effecting structural change will in some way have an impact on public policy.

Trends by Social Justice Field

Social justice-related giving spans all areas of foundation activity, from human rights to the environment to the arts.[5]

♦ Economic and community development topped 2006 social justice priorities

♦ Support for economic and community development grew faster than for other social justice fields

♦ Human rights and civil liberties and economic and community development led by shares of number of grants

♦ Support declined for social science research, public affairs, and educational reform and access

For independent, corporate, community, and grantmaking operating foundations included in the 2006 grants sample, three areas commanded at least 10 percent of social justice dollars—economic and community development (30.5 percent), human rights and civil liberties (13.8 percent), and health care access and affordability (13.4 percent) (Figure 4-5 and Table 4-7).

By comparison, an examination of the shares of number of social justice grants—which are not affected by exceptionally large awards—shows somewhat different grantmaking priorities. For example, while economic and community development accounted for by far the largest share of grant dollars (30.5 percent), human rights and civil liberties benefited from a nearly identical share of grants (18.6 percent and 18.5 percent, respectively). Similarly, housing and shelter, which ranked fifth by grant dollars, moved up to third based on share of number of grants (15.6 percent).

The variation in ranking by grant dollars and grants generally reflects differences in the average size of grants awarded in a field. For example, grants for economic and community development, educational reform and access, health care access and affordability, and international affairs, peace, and conflict resolution were

TABLE 4-7 | Social Justice Giving by Major Field and Subcategories, 2006

Field	Amount	%	No. of Grants	%
Economic and Community Development	**$701,718,570**	**30.5**	**2,841**	**18.6**
Economic Development	622,405,222	27.1	2,060	13.5
Community/Neighborhood Development	70,083,860	3.0	646	4.2
Management and Technical Aid	3,618,350	0.2	57	0.4
Other	5,611,138	0.2	78	0.5
Human Rights and Civil Liberties	**$316,978,659**	**13.8**	**2,815**	**18.5**
Human Rights	235,573,694	10.2	1,916	12.6
Reproductive Rights	27,792,287	1.2	199	1.3
Civil Liberties	22,665,867	1.0	255	1.7
Race/Intergroup Relations	16,238,434	0.7	281	1.8
Other	14,708,377	0.6	164	1.1
Health Care Access and Affordability	**$307,199,291**	**13.4**	**1,288**	**8.4**
Health Care Access and Quality	115,438,301	5.0	537	3.5
Reproductive Health Care Access	59,307,906	2.6	199	1.3
Health Care Cost and Financing	54,261,627	2.4	194	1.2
Mental Health Care Access	17,706,985	0.8	87	0.6
Public Health	60,484,472	2.6	271	1.8
Educational Reform and Access	**$174,489,423**	**7.6**	**898**	**5.9**
Elementary and Secondary	115,531,527	5.0	643	4.2
Higher and Graduate Education	41,894,531	1.8	161	1.1
Other	17,063,365	0.7	94	0.6
Housing and Shelter	**$172,661,342**	**7.5**	**2,429**	**15.6**
Housing Development	153,478,833	6.7	2,133	13.6
Other	19,182,509	0.8	296	1.9
Human Services	**$122,258,944**	**5.3**	**1,248**	**8.2**
International Affairs, Peace, and Conflict Resolution	**$115,762,583**	**5.0**	**519**	**3.4**
Civic Engagement	**$82,732,053**	**3.6**	**592**	**3.9**
Citizen Participation	54,942,197	2.4	400	2.6
Election Regulation and Financing	5,357,761	0.2	44	0.3
Leadership Development	22,432,095	1.0	148	1.0
Crime and Justice	**$81,256,506**	**3.5**	**938**	**6.2**
Legal Services	36,779,337	1.6	611	4.0
Administration of Justice/Courts	21,613,738	0.9	151	1.0
Other	22,863,431	1.0	176	1.2
Environment and Environmental Justice	**$43,442,417**	**1.9**	**382**	**2.5**
Employment Development and Rights	**$42,680,791**	**1.9**	**383**	**2.5**
Public Affairs	**$42,552,952**	**1.8**	**331**	**2.2**
Government Financing and Administration	20,560,073	0.9	157	1.0
Policy and Reform—Multipurpose	4,445,347	0.2	62	0.4
Welfare Policy and Reform	2,061,300	0.1	23	0.2
Other	15,486,232	0.7	89	0.6
Arts, Culture, and Media	**$36,365,580**	**1.6**	**251**	**1.6**
Social Science Research	**$34,253,339**	**1.5**	**199**	**1.3**
Other	**$26,410,233**	**1.1**	**188**	**1.2**
Total	$2,300,762,683	100.0	15,302	100.0

Source: The Foundation Center, *Social Justice Grantmaking II*, 2009. Based on all grants of $10,000 or more awarded by a sample of 871 larger foundations.

FIGURE 4-5 **Social Justice Giving by Major Fields, 2006**

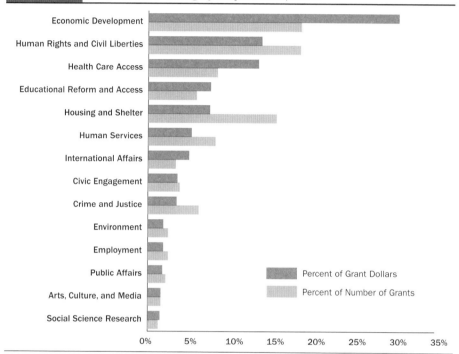

Source: The Foundation Center, *Social Justice Grantmaking II*, 2009. Based on all grants of $10,000 or more awarded by a sample of 749 larger foundations for 2002 and 871 for 2006. Excludes giving by operating foundations.

far larger on average than in other fields (Table 4-8). However, these amounts can be skewed by a handful of exceptionally large grants. The median grant amount—which reflects the grant amount that falls midway between the smallest and largest grant—is often a better measure of the typical grant size in a field. Based on the median social justice grant amount, social science research, health care access and affordability, and educational reform and access led. In contrast, the median grant amount in the following four categories fell below the overall median of $45,000 for the social justice sample—human rights and civil liberties, crime and justice, housing and shelter, and arts, culture, and media.

Foundations increased their support for all but three of the major social justice fields between 2002 and 2006, although rates of growth differed substantially.

FIGURE 4-6 **Change in Social Justice Giving by Major Fields, 2002 and 2006**

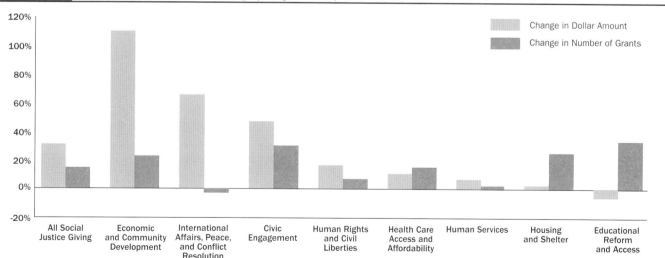

Source: The Foundation Center, *Social Justice Grantmaking II*, 2009. Based on all grants of $10,000 or more awarded by a sample of 749 larger foundations for 2002 and 871 for 2006. Includes subject areas accounting for at least 5 percent of grant dollars in 2006.

TABLE 4-8 — Average and Median Social Justice Grant Amount, 2006

Field	Average Grant Amount	Median Grant Amount[1]
Economic and Community Development	$246,997	$46,000
Health Care Access and Affordability	238,509	75,000
International Affairs, Peace, and Conflict Resolution	223,049	50,000
Educational Reform and Access	194,309	65,000
Social Science Research	172,127	100,000
Arts, Culture, and Media	144,883	30,000
Civic Engagement	139,750	50,000
Public Affairs	128,559	50,000
Environment and Environmental Justice	113,724	50,000
Human Rights and Civil Liberties	112,603	40,000
Employment Development and Rights	111,438	50,000
Human Services	97,964	45,000
Crime and Justice	86,627	35,000
Housing and Shelter	71,083	25,000
All Social Justice Grants	$150,357	$45,000

Source: The Foundation Center, Social Justice Grantmaking II, 2009. Based on all grants of $10,000 or more awarded by a sample of 871 larger foundations.
[1]Within each field, grants were ranked by size, and the grant figure at the midpoint represented the median.

FIGURE 4-7 — Social Justice Giving by Subject and Foundation Type, 2006

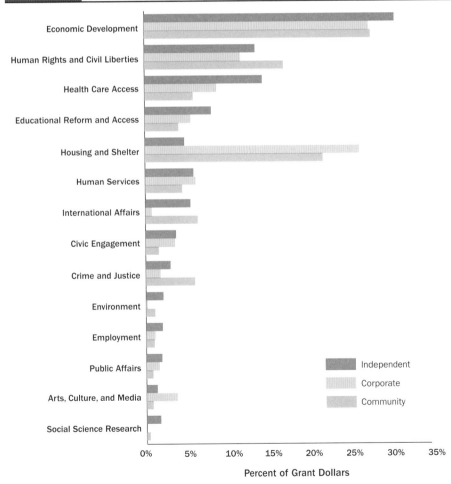

Source: The Foundation Center, Social Justice Grantmaking II, 2009. Based on all grants of $10,000 or more awarded by a sample of 871 larger foundations.

Figure 4-6 and Table 4-9 show the changes in social justice grant dollars and grants between 2002 and 2006, with six of the fields realizing above-average growth. Social justice funders more than doubled their giving for two subject areas: economic and community development (up 109.7 percent) and arts, culture, and the media, including efforts to increase the participation of underserved and minority populations (up 101.2 percent). Other fields experiencing above-average growth included international affairs, peace, and conflict resolution (up 65.4 percent), civic engagement (up 47 percent), crime and justice (up 37.8 percent), and the environment and environmental justice (up 31.5 percent). By comparison, some areas experienced declines in grant dollars, including social science research (down 40.4 percent), public affairs—including support for welfare policy reform and multipurpose policy reform (down 15.7 percent)—and educational reform and access (down 6.2 percent).

A different picture of social justice funding emerges based on a review of changes in the number of social justice grants awarded. Three areas led, with each benefiting from a roughly one-third increase in number of grants—educational reform and access (up 33.6 percent), crime and justice (up 33.2 percent), and civic engagement (up 30.1 percent)—compared to a 14.6 percent growth rate for all social justice grants. Other fields posting above-average growth in grants included housing and shelter (up 25.3 percent), economic and community development (up 22.7 percent), arts, culture, and media (up 15.7 percent), and health care access and affordability (up 15.3 percent). Conversely, three fields experienced decreases in the number of social justice grants they received: social science research (down 21 percent), public affairs (down 9.3 percent), and employment development and rights (down 2.8 percent).

The next section of this chapter provides a more detailed analysis of each of the 14 major social justice fields in 2006, and of the changes in funding since 2002. Where appropriate, it highlights differences in funding priorities by foundation type (Figure 4-7) and identifies the leading funders that had the greatest impact on grantmaking trends during this period (Figure 4-8).

TABLE 4-9	Change in Social Justice Giving by Major Fields, 2002 to 2006					
	Grant Dollars			No. of Grants		
Field	2002	2006	% Change	2002	2006	% Change
Economic and Community Development	$334,646,602	$701,718,570	109.7	2,315	2,841	22.7
Human Rights and Civil Liberties	272,369,392	316,978,659	16.4	2,628	2,815	7.1
Health Care Access and Affordability	277,680,945	307,199,291	10.6	1,117	1,288	15.3
Educational Reform and Access	186,112,452	174,489,423	-6.2	672	898	33.6
Housing and Shelter	168,358,657	172,661,342	2.6	1,938	2,429	25.3
Human Services	114,444,124	122,258,944	6.8	1,218	1,248	2.5
International Affairs, Peace, and Conflict Resolution	70,006,575	115,762,583	65.4	535	519	-3.0
Civic Engagement	56,274,293	82,732,053	47.0	455	592	30.1
Crime and Justice	58,961,607	81,256,506	37.8	704	938	33.2
Environment and Environmental Justice	33,028,471	43,442,417	31.5	376	382	1.6
Employment Development and Rights	42,459,895	42,680,791	0.5	394	383	-2.8
Public Affairs	50,454,645	42,552,952	-15.7	365	331	-9.3
Arts, Culture, and Media	18,077,736	36,365,580	101.2	217	251	15.7
Social Science Research	57,465,690	34,253,339	-40.4	252	199	-21.0
Other	19,195,562	26,410,233	37.6	169	188	11.2
Total	$1,759,536,646	$2,300,762,683	30.8	13,355	15,302	14.6

Source: The Foundation Center, *Social Justice Grantmaking II*, 2009. Based on all grants of $10,000 or more awarded by a sample of 749 larger foundations for 2002 and 871 for 2006.

FIGURE 4-8	Comparison of Social Justice Giving by Leading Social Justice Grantmakers, 2006

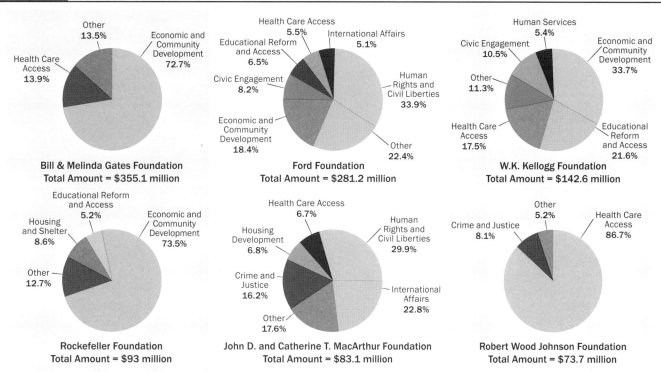

Source: The Foundation Center, *Social Justice Grantmaking II*, 2009. Based on all grants of $10,000 or more.
Note: Other includes fields representing less than 5 percent of grant dollars.

Economic and Community Development

Economic and community development captures support for efforts in the urban and rural United States that increase the economic opportunities, rights, and financial stability of disadvantaged groups and improve the physical condition of their communities. Giving in this area also supports international economic and agricultural development benefiting the developing world.

- ◆ Economic and community development captured the largest share of social justice funding

- ◆ Support for economic and community development more than doubled between 2002 and 2006

- ◆ The Bill & Melinda Gates foundation provided more than one-third of grant dollars in 2006

Economic and community development continued to account for the largest share of support among all social justice funding categories. Close to 31 percent of social justice grant dollars in 2006 funded efforts to increase economic opportunity and improve communities. This area also benefited from the largest share of number of grants (18.6 percent)— although it virtually tied human rights and civil liberties for this distinction (18.5 percent).

Support for economic and community development projects more than doubled from $334.6 million to

$701.7 million between 2002 and 2006. This increase was more than triple the roughly 31 percent rise in social justice funding overall.

Top Funders

Led by the Bill & Melinda Gates Foundation, the top ten funders of economic and community development contributed the vast majority of the funding (Table 4-10). Together, these foundations accounted for close to three-quarters (72.2 percent) of grant dollars in 2006. Funding by the Gates Foundation alone provided almost 37 percent of grant dollars for economic and community development, after its giving in the area increased from $2.2 million in 2002 to more than $258 million. This increase resulted in large part from the launch of the foundation's new Global Development Program in 2006. Other funders accounting for at least 5 percent of economic and community

---

FIGURE 4-9 **Economic and Community Development, Giving to Subcategories, 2006**

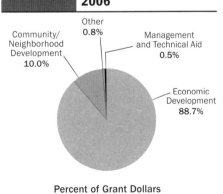

Community/
Neighborhood
Development
10.0%

Other
0.8%

Management
and Technical Aid
0.5%

Economic
Development
88.7%

Percent of Grant Dollars

Source: The Foundation Center, *Social Justice Grantmaking II*, 2009. Based on all grants of $10,000 or more awarded by a sample of 871 larger foundations.

TABLE 4-10 **Top 10 Economic and Community Development Funders, 2006**

Foundation Name	State	Grant Dollars	%	No. of Grants	%
1. Bill & Melinda Gates Foundation	WA	$258,024,805	36.8	42	1.5
2. Rockefeller Foundation	NY	68,324,260	9.7	39	1.4
3. Ford Foundation	NY	51,630,756	7.4	164	5.8
4. W.K. Kellogg Foundation	MI	49,195,604	7.0	113	4.0
5. Northwest Area Foundation	MN	30,617,842	4.4	24	0.8
6. Citi Foundation	NY	11,222,535	1.6	112	3.9
7. Starr Foundation	NY	10,735,000	1.5	8	0.3
8. William and Flora Hewlett Foundation	CA	10,717,600	1.5	32	1.1
9. Annie E. Casey Foundation	MD	8,029,676	1.1	73	2.6
10. San Diego Foundation	CA	7,944,563	1.1	11	0.4
Subtotal for Top 10		**$506,442,641**	**72.2**	**618**	**21.8**
Total		$701,718,570	100.0	2,841	100.0

Source: The Foundation Center, *Social Justice Grantmaking II*, 2009. Based on all grants of $10,000 or more awarded by a sample of 871 larger foundations.

development giving in 2006 included the Rockefeller (9.7 percent), Ford (7.4 percent), W.K. Kellogg (7.0 percent), and Northwest Area (4.4 percent) foundations.

Giving Trends

The vast majority of funding for economic and community development focuses on promoting large- and small-scale economic development opportunities in developing countries and the United States (Figure 4-9). Efforts to encourage neighborhood development and revitalization and the building of strong communities benefited from the next–largest share of giving in this category, although support for this purpose was down from 2002. In fact, with the exception of economic development, all subcategories in this area posted a decrease in grant dollars between 2002 and 2006.

Economic Development. Support for international development, urban and rural development in the United States, and funding to ensure the financial security of those least well off accounted for almost nine out of 10 grant dollars awarded for economic and community development. Giving totaled $622.4 million in 2006, more than triple the $206.7 million reported in 2002.

Support for U.S.-based international programs or for organizations located outside of the United States represented more than two-thirds of giving (69.6 percent) in this area—compared to 39.5 percent in the overall social justice sample. In 2006, a funding partnership between the

Bill & Melinda Gates Foundation and Rockefeller Foundation to introduce the "Green Revolution" to Africa was a key factor raising the level of giving for international economic development. Together these foundations awarded $150 million to the Nairobi-based Alliance for a Green Revolution to help African farmers increase their productivity. As previously noted, the $50 million grant awarded by Rockefeller ranked as the largest social justice grant in 2006.

Support to strengthen the capacity and outreach efforts of microfinance programs in developing countries and the United States was also a growing area of interest of foundations in 2006. A prominent example is the Bill & Melinda Gates Foundation's $6.3 million grant to MicroSave India to optimize the provision of micro-finance products and improve the outreach and efficiency to reach greater scale in India. Other funders such as the Citi, Ford, W.K. Kellogg, and Charles Stewart Mott foundations also awarded at least one grant for this purpose.

Domestically, two of the largest grants for economic development were awarded by the Northwest Area Foundation as part of its Ventures Program, which supports community poverty reduction strategies that create pathways out of poverty for the most disadvantaged. In 2006, the foundation's support included grants to two Native American tribes— $10 million to the North Dakota-based Turtle Mountain Band of Chippewa Indians and $9.5 million to the South Dakota-based Cheyenne River Sioux Tribe.

"In 2006, we established the Global Development Program to increase opportunities for people in the developing world to lift themselves out of hunger and poverty….[T]he program's first year focused on an ambitious partnership with the Rockefeller Foundation to help African farmers increase their productivity and on a series of innovative efforts to bring financial services to poor people in Africa and Asia who haven't had access to them before."

— The Bill & Melinda Gates Foundation Annual Report

Community/Neighborhood Development. Funding for neighborhood development and for community organizing to build strong, sustainable communities accounted for one in 10 economic and community development grant dollars in 2006. However, funding was down 15.3 percent, from $82.7 million in 2002 to $70.1 million. This decline in part reflects the absence of a grant similar in scale to the $40 million grant awarded by the Price Family Charitable Fund to the San Diego Revitalization Corporation in 2002. By comparison, there was a significant increase in the number of grants in this area, showing a strong level of commitment by several funders to supporting a wide range of community development organizations. Among these grants were six awards from the Charles Stewart Mott Foundation made through its Intermediary Support for Organizing Communities initiative, which seeks to provide technical assistance and regranting to emerging community-based organizations serving low-income neighborhoods.

Management and Technical Aid. Support focused on providing management and technical assistance for economic and community development projects decreased considerably between 2002 and 2006. Grant dollars were down about 90 percent, and the number of grants decreased nearly 67 percent. Awards in this subcategory tended to be smaller than other economic and community development grants. The single largest management and technical aid grant tracked in 2006 was a $425,000 award for general operating support to Philadelphia-based Public/Private Ventures, a national nonprofit organization whose mission is to improve the effectiveness of social policies, programs, and community initiatives, especially as they affect youth and young adults.

Spotlight on Selected Grants

NORTHWEST AREA FOUNDATION awarded $4.7 million to the Texas-based **Rural Development and Finance Corporation** to increase the capacity of low-income rural Latinos to undertake poverty reduction work.

CITI FOUNDATION awarded $700,000 to Virginia-based Charities Aid Foundation America for the **Indian School of Microfinance for Women**, based in Ahmedabad, India.

FORD FOUNDATION awarded $350,000 to Washington State-based **Shorebank Enterprise Group Pacific** to scale up delivery of loan and community development services for rural and Native American communities in Oregon.

SOCIAL JUSTICE GRANTMAKING FOR COMMUNITY ORGANIZING

Community organizing continues to be an important tool in efforts to advance social justice. Funders included in the Foundation Center's grants sample provided nearly $73 million in social justice-related support for community organizing in 2006, or 3.2 percent of overall social justice giving.

Support for community organizing reached most fields, although close to half of dollars ($33.3 million) focused on the broad goal of strengthening community coalitions serving the economically disadvantaged. Among grants for this purpose was the Otto Bremer Foundation's $50,000 award to the People Escaping Poverty Project for community organizing, leadership development, collaborative building and support, and technology; and the Charles Stewart Mott Foundation's $370,000 grant to the Center for Community Change to improve the ability of low-income residents to shape programs that affect their lives by building the field of community organizing in targeted regions of the United States.

Specific fields benefiting from notable shares of community organizing grant dollars in 2006 included health care access and affordability (13.3 percent), educational reform (9.4 percent), human rights (8.4 percent), human services (6.9 percent), and environmental justice (6.8 percent). Among community organizing grants specifically related to health care, the Richard and Rhoda Goldman Fund awarded $50,000 to Physicians for Reproductive Choice and Health for the Bay Area Community Organizing Project to support a local network of pro-choice physicians that advocate for reproductive rights and health. Grants also focused on multiple fields, such as the New York Foundation's $42,500 award to Centro Hispano Cuzcatlan to organize community residents in Eastern Queens on housing, immigrants' rights, and local land-use issues.

Human Rights and Civil Liberties

Human rights and civil liberties encompasses support for efforts to ensure human rights and civil liberties in the United States, as well as international human rights. It also captures giving to ensure women's reproductive rights and to enhance understanding and appreciation of human diversity.

- ◆ Support for human rights and civil liberties grew more slowly than overall social justice giving between 2002 and 2006

- ◆ The Ford Foundation provided almost one-third of grant dollars

Human rights and civil liberties accounted for the second–largest share of social justice grant dollars in 2006 but roughly matched economic and community development by share of number of grants (18.5 percent versus 18.6 percent). Between 2002 and 2006, grant dollars grew at a slower-than-average 16.4 percent, from $272.4 million to $317 million, while the number of grants increased 7.1 percent, from 2,628 to 2,815.

Top Funders

The Ford Foundation dominated funding for human rights and civil liberties, providing close to one-third of all giving (Table 4-11). Ford's

support rose to $95.5 million in 2006, up by $12.8 million from 2002. The foundation's largest grant in this area was a $4.3 million award to New York City-based Public Interest Projects for the Fulfilling the Dream Fund, a donor collaborative designed to increase the resources available to strengthen and defend affirmative action.

The top 10 human rights and civil liberties funders accounted for more than half (55.7 percent) of 2006 support and just over one-quarter of the number of grants. In addition to Ford, three foundations provided at least $10 million for human rights and civil liberties, including the John D. and Catherine T. MacArthur Foundation ($24.8 million), Bill & Melinda Gates Foundation ($10.9 million), and Susan Thompson Buffett Foundation ($10.3 million). The Gates Foundation provided the largest grant in this area in the latest sample—a $10 million award to the

---

FIGURE 4-10 Human Rights and Civil Liberties, Giving to Subcategories, 2006

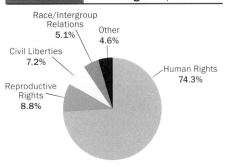

Race/Intergroup Relations 5.1%
Other 4.6%
Civil Liberties 7.2%
Reproductive Rights 8.8%
Human Rights 74.3%

Percent of Grant Dollars

Source: The Foundation Center, *Social Justice Grantmaking II*, 2009. Based on all grants of $10,000 or more awarded by a sample of 871 larger foundations.

TABLE 4-11 Top 10 Human Rights and Civil Liberties Funders, 2006

Foundation Name	State	Grant Dollars	%	No. of Grants	%
1. Ford Foundation	NY	$95,451,318	30.1	319	11.3
2. John D. and Catherine T. MacArthur Foundation	IL	24,846,000	7.8	74	2.6
3. Bill & Melinda Gates Foundation	WA	10,850,630	3.4	3	0.1
4. Susan Thompson Buffett Foundation	NE	10,250,934	3.2	11	0.4
5. Open Society Institute	NY	7,761,434	2.4	74	2.6
6. Evelyn and Walter Haas, Jr. Fund	CA	7,560,750	2.4	73	2.6
7. Peninsula Community Foundation	CA	6,201,837	2.0	26	0.9
8. Gill Foundation	CO	4,614,100	1.5	100	3.6
9. Marguerite Casey Foundation	WA	4,472,166	1.4	25	0.0
10. JEHT Foundation[1]	NY	4,411,529	1.4	42	1.5
Subtotal for Top 10		**$176,420,698**	**55.7**	**747**	**26.5**
Total		$316,978,659	100.0	2,815	100.0

Source: The Foundation Center, *Social Justice Grantmaking II*, 2009. Based on all grants of $10,000 or more awarded by a sample of 871 larger foundations.
[1]The foundation ceased operation in January 2009.

Geneva-based United Nations High Commissioner for Refugees to facilitate the safe repatriation of Sudanese refugees.

Giving Trends

Among the five human rights and civil liberties subcategories, only human rights benefited from growth in funding between 2002 and 2006. Moreover, support for human rights in the United States and in other countries accounted for the majority of giving for human rights and civil liberties (Figure 4-10).

Human Rights. Funding for human rights, including the rights of specific population groups, accounted for about three-quarters (74.3 percent) of all human rights and civil liberties giving in 2006. Grant dollars totaled $235.6 million, up by almost two-fifths from $170.2 million in 2002. Funding in this area included the Evelyn and Walter Haas, Jr. Fund's $350,000 grant to the Massachusetts-based Proteus Fund to build state and local grassroots constituencies that support same-sex marriage and oppose efforts to curtail lesbian and gay civil rights.

Half of grant dollars and close to 38 percent of grants for human rights targeted internationally focused human rights programs in the United States and overseas. Among awards providing this support was the John D. and Catherine T. MacArthur Foundation's $450,000 program support grant to the Australia-based Asia Pacific Forum of National Human Rights Institutions.

Reproductive Rights. Giving to ensure the reproductive rights of women represented 8.8 percent of human rights and civil liberties funding in 2006. Both grant dollars and the number of grants decreased between 2002 and 2006 (8.3 percent and 18.4 percent, respectively). The three largest grants in this subcategory for 2006 were awarded to reproductive rights organizations by the Susan Thompson Buffett Foundation:

$3.1 million to the Istanbul-based Willows Foundation, $1.5 million to the DC-based Religious Coalition for Reproductive Choice, and $1.1 million to the Mexico City-based Equidad de Genero: Ciudadania, Trabajo y Familia. (See "Health Care Access and Affordability" for details on funding to ensure access to reproductive health care.)

Civil Liberties. Support to ensure a wide range of civil liberties in the United States commanded a 7.2 percent share of human rights and civil liberties funding in 2006. This $22.7 million total was down by more than one-third from 2002. However, the number of grants grew by 7.1 percent—although this was half the average rate of growth for social justice giving overall. Civil liberties support was concentrated around advocacy issues ($10.8 million) and first amendment rights ($4.3 million). For example, the Ford Foundation awarded $250,000 to Alliance for Justice for opinion research on the enforcement of constitutional rights. Other grants included support for a variety of purposes, such as freedom of religion, freedom of information, death penalty issues, right to privacy, right to life, right to die, and right to due process.

Race/Intergroup Relations. Funding to increase understanding and collaboration among racial, ethnic, religious, and other groups accounted for 5.1 percent of human rights and civil liberties grant dollars in 2006, down from 10.4 percent in 2002. Grant dollars targeting these activities declined 42.6 percent during this period. The Ford Foundation awarded the largest grant for race/intergroup relations in 2006—a $1.1 million award to the New York City-based Anti-Defamation League of B'nai B'rith to scale-up the online platform for delivering the teacher education programs of the World of Difference Institute, followed by the Allstate Foundation's $1 million grant to the Atlanta-based Boys and Girls Clubs of America for the Tolerance and Inclusion program.

Other. Support for the remaining human rights and civil liberties activities jumped from $8.4 million in 2002 to $14.7 million in 2006. This increase was largely the result of increased funding for voter education and rights, which reached $11.9 million. Among the largest grants for this purpose was a $400,000 award from the James Irvine Foundation to the Los Angeles-based Southwest Voter Registration Education Project to conduct nonpartisan voter education and mobilization activities among Latinos in low-income communities in Los Angeles, Riverside, and San Bernardino Counties, as part of the California Votes Initiative.

Spotlight on Selected Grants

*DAVID AND LUCILE PACKARD FOUNDATION awarded $250,000 to the **American Civil Liberties Union (ACLU) Foundation of Northern California** for its Reproductive Rights Project.*

*ROCHESTER AREA COMMUNITY FOUNDATION awarded $50,000 to New York-based **Odyssey of Humanity** to implement the next phase of the Rochester Mosaic Partnership, which seeks to build trust and tolerance among people of different races and ethnicities.*

*OTTO BREMER FOUNDATION awarded $29,000 to Minnesota-based **Concordia University** for the Race Education through Values Engagement, Advocacy and Leadership (REVEAL) Program, which works to increase cultural competence.*

SOCIAL JUSTICE GRANTMAKING FOR HUMAN RIGHTS AND CIVIL LIBERTIES

◆ **More than one-quarter of funding provided primary or secondary support for human rights and civil liberties**

Many social justice grantmakers view the protection and advancement of the rights of disadvantaged and vulnerable populations as a core component of their missions. The San Francisco-based Evelyn and Walter Haas, Jr. Foundation, for example, states that "a just and caring society [is] measured by how well it provides fundamental rights and opportunities to all people."

In 2006, almost 14 percent of overall social justice grant dollars ($317 million) and close to 19 percent of grants (2,815) provided primary support for human rights or civil liberties. (See "Human Rights and Civil Liberties" for further details.) However, these figures do not capture grants whose secondary purpose targeted human rights. For example,

a grant to reduce health care disparities for immigrant populations would have a primary purpose of "health," since its main goal was to improve the health outcomes of patients, but a secondary purpose of "human rights," reflecting its emphasis on providing equal access to quality health care.

When secondary coding was included, support for human rights and civil liberties increased to close to 28 percent of grant dollars ($635 million) and more than one-third of the grants (5,138) in 2006. Fields reporting the largest amounts of human rights support based on primary or secondary coding were economic and community development ($82.3 million) and health care access and affordability ($46.7 million). Regardless, all social justice fields received grants that included secondary coding for human rights or civil liberties, reinforcing the centrality of advancing rights among many social justice funders.

Health Care Access and Affordability

Health care access and affordability encompasses efforts to improve the health of disadvantaged and disenfranchised groups through support for organizations and programs seeking to improve public health, increase health care affordability, accessibility, and quality, and reduce substance abuse. Funding in this area also seeks to ensure access to reproductive health care and mental health care.

- ◆ Support for health care access and affordability rose modestly between 2002 and 2006

- ◆ Robert Wood Johnson, California Endowment, and Gates provided more than half of giving in 2006

- ◆ Health care access and quality accounted for largest share of giving

Funding for health care access and affordability nearly matched human rights and civil liberties by share of 2006 social justice grant dollars (13.4 percent versus 13.8 percent). Grant dollars for the field rose much more slowly than overall social justice giving between 2002 and 2006 (up 10.6 percent), with actual grant dollars reaching $307.2 million in the latter year. In contrast, the number of health-related grants rose 15.3 percent, just ahead of the overall sample.

Top Funders

The three largest funders in this area—the Robert Wood Johnson Foundation (RWJF), California Endowment, and Bill & Melinda Gates Foundation—provided more than half of all giving for health care access and affordability in 2006 (Table 4-12). Although RWJF was the top funder in both 2002 and 2006, its giving dropped from $132.6 million to $60.8 million in the most recent year. Still, the foundation awarded 12 grants of $1 million or more in this area, including an $8 million grant to the University of New Mexico Foundation for the endowment of the Robert Wood Johnson Foundation Center for Health Policy. The Center will contribute to the development and implementation of national health policies by increasing the number of Hispanic and Native American scholars who can engage in health care policy debates as leaders.

FIGURE 4-11 **Health Care Access and Affordability, Giving to Subcategories, 2006**

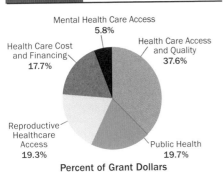

Mental Health Care Access
5.8%

Health Care Cost and Financing
17.7%

Health Care Access and Quality
37.6%

Reproductive Healthcare Access
19.3%

Public Health
19.7%

Percent of Grant Dollars

Source: The Foundation Center, *Social Justice Grantmaking II*, 2009. Based on all grants of $10,000 or more awarded by a sample of 871 larger foundations.

TABLE 4-12 **Top 10 Health Care Access and Affordability Funders, 2006**

Foundation Name	State	Grant Dollars	%	No. of Grants	%
1. Robert Wood Johnson Foundation	NJ	$60,807,171	20.0	149	11.6
2. California Endowment	CA	53,942,961	17.7	210	16.4
3. Bill & Melinda Gates Foundation	WA	49,251,487	16.2	11	0.9
4. W.K. Kellogg Foundation	MI	24,880,224	8.2	61	4.8
5. Ford Foundation	NY	15,492,021	5.1	37	2.9
6. California Wellness Foundation	CA	13,598,000	4.5	5	0.4
7. WellPoint Foundation	CA	10,537,200	3.5	37	2.9
8. Commonwealth Fund	NY	5,832,425	1.9	20	1.6
9. John D. and Catherine T. MacArthur Foundation	IL	5,547,000	1.8	60	4.7
10. David and Lucile Packard Foundation	CA	4,327,500	1.4	13	1.0
Subtotal for Top 10		**$244,215,989**	**80.4**	**603**	**47.1**
Total		$307,199,291	100.0	1,288	100.0

Source: The Foundation Center, *Social Justice Grantmaking II*, 2009. Based on all grants of $10,000 or more awarded by a sample of 871 larger foundations.

The second-ranked California Endowment awarded $53.9 million for 210 grants—the largest number of grants in this category. Their 2006 funding included a $616,000 grant to the Oakland-based Alameda-Contra Costa Medical Association for their Language Access initiative. This program supports coalition capacity building and the development of collaborative models that improve language access services in health care settings for limited-English-speaking residents of Alameda County.

Only four grants included in the 2006 social justice sample were for at least $25 million, and these included the third-ranked Bill & Melinda Gates Foundation's $25.2 million award to the Bangladesh Rural Advance Commission (BRAC) to demonstrate an effective and transferable program model for improving maternal, newborn, and child health in poor urban communities of developing countries. Other top-ranked funders in this area that reported at least $10 million in grant dollars included the W.K. Kellogg ($24.9 million), Ford ($15.5 million), California Wellness ($13.6 million), and WellPoint ($10.5 million) foundations.

Giving Trends

More than one-third of 2006 funding targeted to health care access and affordability supported efforts to increase access and improve quality (Figure 4-11). Additional one-fifth shares of health dollars supported efforts to improve public health, ensure access to reproductive health care, and address health care costs and financing.

The balance of giving supported efforts to reduce substance abuse and expand access to mental health care. Among these subcategories, support for public health issues and access to reproductive health care increased at a faster-than-average rate between 2002 and 2006, while grant dollars for the expansion of heath care coverage and access to mental health care declined.

Health Care Access and Quality. Funding to increase access to health care for disadvantaged and disenfranchised populations and improve its quality for these groups accounted for well over one-third (37.6 percent) of health-related social justice giving in 2006. Although representing the largest share of funding, actual grant dollars rose a relatively modest 14.1 percent, from $101.2 million in 2002 to $115.4 million in 2006. The W.K. Kellogg Foundation awarded five grants of $1 million or more in support of access to health care, including a $1.3 million award to the Children's Health Fund to improve the health of low-income children residing in communities with a shortage of health and dental professionals by addressing transportation issues.

Public Health. Funding for social justice-related public health policy soared between 2002 and 2006, from $22.6 million to $60.5 million. The number of grants also increased, from 152 to 271. Contributing to this rise was the Bill & Melinda Gates Foundation's $10.7 million grant to DC-based ActionAid USA to develop the capacity of NGOs working within Europe to increase the

> "Good health means more than just good health care. Several social factors—poverty, race, education and housing—play a critical role in the health and health care problems that affect society's most vulnerable and often-neglected people."
>
> — Robert Wood Johnson Foundation Annual Report

interest and support of governments and institutions in achieving the global health Millennium Development Goals.

Reproductive Health Care Access. Support for ensuring access to reproductive health care grew by more than half from 2002 to 2006, well above the average for the sample. Similar to 2002, the vast majority of funding focused on work outside the United States, such as the $25.2 million Gates Foundation grant to BRAC (noted above) and the John D. and Catherine T. MacArthur Foundation's $470,000 grant to the Mexico City-based Sociedad Mexicana pro Derechos de la Mujer to strengthen the leadership capacity of indigenous women in an effort to decrease maternal mortality and improve the population's reproductive health. Funding within the United States included a $120,000 grant from the Richard and Rhoda Goldman

Fund to the NARAL Pro-Choice California Foundation for the Activist Empowerment Initiative, which supports mobilizing rural populations in Northern California counties to advocate for expanded reproductive health access. (See "Human Rights and Civil Liberties" for details on funding for reproductive rights.)

Health Care Cost and Financing. Grants addressing health care costs and financing represented close to one-fifth of health-related social justice giving in the 2006 sample, down from a roughly one-third share of funding in 2002. Nonetheless, the number of grants grew by 14.1 percent—matching the overall rate of increase. Most funding in this area targeted efforts to provide health insurance to low-income uninsured populations, including a $296,966 grant from the Michael and Susan Dell Foundation to the Daughters of Charity Health Services of Austin for the Insure-A-Kid School

Outreach program, which provides free or low-cost health insurance for Texas children.

Mental Health Care Access. Support for policy-related efforts to reduce substance abuse among the disadvantaged and disenfranchised and to improve broad public access to mental health care decreased by nearly one-third in 2006. The Robert Wood Johnson Foundation was the major funder in this area, awarding 22 grants. Among these awards were four made through the foundation's Reclaiming our Futures: Communities Helping Teens Overcome Drugs, Alcohol and Crime program, which seeks to develop new service delivery models that integrate comprehensive services into the juvenile justice system and promotes the creation of community-based systems of care for substance-abusing youthful offenders.

Spotlight on Selected Grants

CALIFORNIA ENDOWMENT awarded $935,476 to **Children Now** for the Health Insurance for Every Californian Media Campaign for work toward achieving health care coverage for all of California's kids by engaging in a statewide public awareness media campaign.

BUSH FOUNDATION awarded $236,431 to the Minnesota-based **Fairview Foundation** to increase immigrant access to medical services by providing skilled interpreters.

ROBERT STERLING CLARK FOUNDATION awarded $100,000 to the New York-based **Institute for Reproductive Health Access** for public education, advocacy, and assistance to advocates in states around the country to promote policy reforms that would facilitate access to emergency contraception.

DOMESTIC VS. INTERNATIONAL SOCIAL JUSTICE GRANTMAKING

◆ **Social justice funders were almost twice as likely as funders overall to provide international support**

◆ **International social justice support more than doubled from 2002 to 2006**

A markedly larger share of social justice grant dollars supported international activities in the latest period. Social justice-related funding for U.S.-based international programs and overseas recipients totaled $908 million in 2006, more than double the $440 million recorded for 2002. As a result, internationally focused social justice funding represented 40 percent of grant dollars in 2006 (Figure 4-I1), compared to the 22 percent of overall grant dollars that provided international support that year.

Most of this growth in grant dollars resulted from exceptionally large awards provided by the Bill & Melinda

Gates and Rockefeller foundations to introduce the "green revolution" to Africa. As a result, the share of number of internationally focused social justice grants remained almost unchanged (20.1 percent).

The domestic and international giving priorities of social justice funders were noticeably different in 2006. Figure 4-I2 shows that by far the largest share of international social justice giving (44.5 percent) supported economic and community development programs, more than double the share for domestic giving (20.5 percent). Human rights and civil liberties commanded the next-largest share of international funding—albeit a far smaller 14.6 percent. The only other fields benefiting from a larger share of international social justice-related funding relative to domestic funding were social science research and environment and environmental justice.

FIGURE 4-I1 Social Justice vs. Overall Domestic and International Giving, 2006

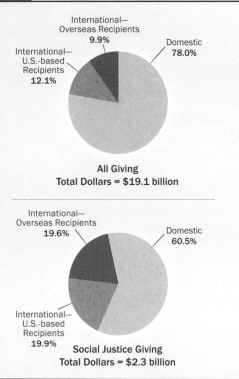

All Giving
Total Dollars = $19.1 billion

Social Justice Giving
Total Dollars = $2.3 billion

Source: The Foundation Center, *Social Justice Grantmaking II,* 2009. Based on all grants of $10,000 or more awarded by a sample of 1,263 larger foundations.

FIGURE 4-I2 Domestic vs. International Social Justice Giving by Major Fields, 2006

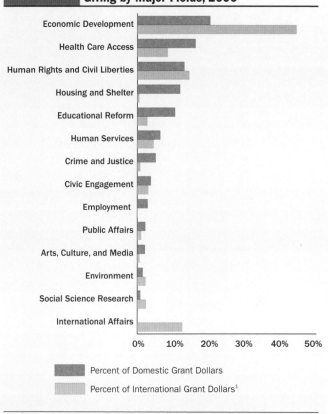

Source: The Foundation Center, *Social Justice Grantmaking II,* 2009. Based on all grants of $10,000 or more awarded by a sample of 871 larger foundations.
[1]Includes support for U.S.-based international programs and recipients in other countries.

Educational Reform and Access

Educational reform and access includes support for efforts to improve elementary and secondary education and retention and diversify faculty at these institutions, improve preparation for post-secondary education, and increase access to post-secondary institutions and ensure the retention and academic success of disadvantaged students.[6]

♦ **Funding for educational reform and access declined between 2002 and 2006**

♦ **Elementary and secondary school reform accounted for two-thirds of grant dollars**

Efforts to reform and provide access to education captured 7.6 percent of social justice funding in 2006, although this share was down from 10.6 percent in 2002. Grant dollars for educational reform and access declined 6.2 percent during this period, making it one of three social justice fields experiencing a reduction. In contrast, the number of grants for educational reform and access grew by one-third— the largest increase in grants reported for any category, and more than double the average for the social justice sample overall. This finding suggests that there continues to be strong interest among social justice funders in this area but fewer very large grants.

Top Funders

The top 10 funders of educational reform and access provided roughly two-thirds of giving in this area in 2006 (Table 4-13). The lead funder, by far, was the W.K. Kellogg Foundation, with giving up from $23.8 million in 2002 to $30.8 million in 2006. Among the 27 grants Kellogg awarded for educational reform was one of the area's largest grants: $6.3 million to the University of North Carolina to reduce gender disparities in the academic achievement of boys of color in early education and promote school success by the third grade.

Both the second- and third-ranked Ford and Bill & Melinda Gates foundations reduced their giving for educational reform and access between 2002 and 2006, contributing to the overall decline. In 2006, Ford's support totaled $18.4 million, down $7.4 million, while Gates awarded $13.4 million, down $36.3 million. Nonetheless, the Ford Foundation awarded the largest number of grants

---

FIGURE 4-12 | **Educational Reform and Access, Giving to Subcategories, 2006**

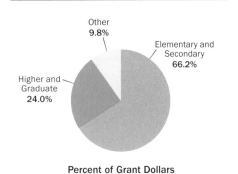

Other
9.8%

Elementary and Secondary
66.2%

Higher and Graduate
24.0%

Percent of Grant Dollars

Source: The Foundation Center, *Social Justice Grantmaking II*, 2009. Based on all grants of $10,000 or more awarded by a sample of 871 larger foundations.

TABLE 4-13 | **Top 10 Educational Reform and Access Funders, 2006**

Foundation Name	State	Grant Dollars	%	No. of Grants	%
1. W.K. Kellogg Foundation	MI	$30,798,007	17.7	27	3.0
2. Ford Foundation	NY	18,397,850	10.5	50	5.6
3. Bill & Melinda Gates Foundation	WA	13,399,133	7.7	18	2.0
4. Lumina Foundation for Education	IN	8,542,400	4.9	47	5.2
5. William and Flora Hewlett Foundation	CA	8,517,000	4.9	22	2.4
6. Charles Stewart Mott Foundation	MI	6,927,729	4.0	30	3.3
7. Carnegie Corporation of New York	NY	5,899,500	3.4	17	1.9
8. Rockefeller Foundation	NY	4,863,888	2.8	10	1.1
9. GE Foundation	CT	4,749,444	2.7	29	3.2
10. Annenberg Foundation	PA	4,719,039	2.7	6	0.7
Subtotal for Top 10		**$106,813,990**	**61.2**	**256**	**28.5**
Total		$174,489,423	100.0	898	100.0

Source: The Foundation Center, *Social Justice Grantmaking II*, 2009. Based on all grants of $10,000 or more awarded by a sample of 871 larger foundations.

for educational reform and access (50), including $3 million to the Atlanta-based Southern Education Foundation for endowment support to increase educational opportunities for African Americans and other low-income people in the South.

The Gates Foundation awarded 18 grants, including a $2.2 million general support grant to the Education Trust, which works for the high academic achievement of all students at all levels, pre-kindergarten through college, and to close the achievement gaps that separate low-income students and students of color from other youth.

Giving Trends

Grantmaking to reform elementary and secondary education dominated funding for educational reform and access in 2006. The balance of giving supported higher and graduate education and other efforts to reform education and to provide equal access for all students (Figure 4-12).

Elementary and Secondary Education. Funding focused on elementary and secondary education represented two-thirds of educational reform and access grant dollars in 2006. Giving totaled $115.5 million—down marginally from 2002—while the number of grants rose by more than half (53.5 percent). Among its funding in this area, the Lumina Foundation for Education awarded several grants aimed at providing pre-collegiate access services to high school students, including African-American males.

Higher and Graduate Education. Giving to increase access to and achieve equity and quality in higher education for underrepresented groups and to improve the outcomes for these students totaled almost one-quarter of educational reform and access grant dollars in 2006. The number of grants grew by 17.5 percent from 2002, although grant dollars were down 18.1 percent. Support included a $400,000 award from the William and Flora Hewlett Foundation to

"Reaching world-class levels of college attainment will require the United States to find ways to assure that dramatically more residents have the opportunity to succeed in higher education."

— Lumina Foundation for Education web site

MDRC for the inclusion of Chaffey College in Opening Doors, a national demonstration project on strategies to increase the persistence rates of disadvantaged community college students; and a $50,000 grant from the Otto Bremer Foundation to the Minnesota Minority Education Partnership to support a statewide college access network and provide organizing and policy work for students of color.

Spotlight on Selected Grants

W.K. KELLOGG FOUNDATION awarded $1.5 million to the Virginia-based **Rural School and Community Trust** to build the capacity of grassroots and community-based organizational leaders to engage in local school transformation in vulnerable rural communities, and to establish a network of rural school supporters who will work to improve education for students throughout North Carolina.

CHARLES STEWART MOTT FOUNDATION awarded $600,000 to the Rhode Island-based **Annenberg Institute for School Reform at Brown University** to evaluate the Education Organizing Study, which seeks to understand the added value of community organizing to school improvement, documenting ways in which community organizing strategies produce concrete educational improvements for low-income children.

GEORGE GUND FOUNDATION awarded $80,000 to the Ohio-based **Shaker Heights City School District** for a program to close the achievement gap between African-American and white students.

Housing and Shelter

Housing and shelter encompasses efforts to provide access to safe, affordable housing for low-income and underserved groups—including support for housing development and advocacy efforts to advance affordable housing, promote housing rights, and create transitional housing for the homeless and families in crisis.

◆ Grant dollars for housing and shelter nearly unchanged between 2002 and 2006

◆ Number of grants increased by one-quarter

Housing and shelter represented 7.5 percent of social justice grant dollars in 2006, down from 9.6 percent in 2002. Grant dollars rose a marginal 2.6 percent during this period, from $168.4 million to $172.7 million. However, the number of grants increased by one-quarter, surpassing the average increase in the social justice sample. Virtually all of the funding for housing focused on domestic projects.

Corporate foundations were strong supporters of housing and shelter. In 2006, corporate funders provided 30.9 percent of the grant dollars and more than half (52.5 percent) of the number of grants in this area. By comparison, corporate foundations accounted for a far more modest 8.8 percent of the dollars and 22.9 percent of grants awarded for social justice overall.

Top Funders

Unlike most other categories of social justice funding, support for housing was not as heavily concentrated among the largest grantmakers. The top 10 funders accounted for a relatively modest 36 percent of the dollars and 35.4 percent of the grants. In addition, no one foundation significantly dominated the category.

The Bank of America Charitable Foundation was new to the list of top 10 housing and shelter grantmakers in 2006 but nonetheless took the top spot, awarding $ 8.7 million—a $6.5 million increase over 2002 (Table 4-14). The foundation's largest housing grant was a $1 million award to Maryland-based Enterprise Community Partners, an organization that helps to build affordable housing for low-income Americans. The second–largest funder, the Rockefeller Foundation, also significantly increased its giving for housing. Its funding climbed to $8 million in 2006, a $7.3 million increase over 2002.

TABLE 4-14 **Top 10 Housing and Shelter Funders, 2006**

Foundation Name	State	Grant Dollars	%	No. of Grants	%
1. Bank of America Charitable Foundation	NC	$8,708,581	5.0	143	5.9
2. Rockefeller Foundation	NY	7,950,000	4.6	8	0.3
3. Citi Foundation	NY	7,289,400	4.2	139	5.7
4. John D. and Catherine T. MacArthur Foundation	IL	6,885,000	4.0	18	0.7
5. Fannie Mae Foundation	DC	6,470,000	3.7	80	3.3
6. Wells Fargo Foundation	CA	5,725,676	3.3	287	11.8
7. Community Foundation Silicon Valley	CA	4,883,234	2.8	19	0.8
8. JPMorgan Chase Foundation	NY	4,856,025	2.8	122	5.0
9. Ford Foundation	NY	4,079,100	2.4	19	0.8
10. Weingart Foundation	CA	3,635,000	2.1	5	0.2
Subtotal for Top 10		**$60,482,016**	**35.0**	**840**	**34.6**
Total		$172,661,342	100.0	2,429	100.0

Source: The Foundation Center, *Social Justice Grantmaking II*, 2009. Based on all grants of $10,000 or more awarded by a sample of 871 larger foundations.

Rockefeller awarded the largest housing grant in the latest sample: $5 million to the New York Acquisition Fund to capitalize the New York City Acquisition Loan Fund, LLC and accelerate and increase development of affordable housing in New York City.

The Wells Fargo Foundation awarded the largest number of grants for housing and shelter in 2006 (287). Its largest housing-related grant was a $106,000 award to the Cook Inlet Housing Authority, a nonprofit dedicated to insuring access to quality housing for a variety of populations, including Alaska Natives and American Indians.

Giving Trends

The vast majority of housing and shelter support targeted housing development, which seeks to create affordable housing for low-income families and other underserved groups. A much smaller share supported assistance to low-income families seeking home ownership, and for housing services and activities advocating equal access to housing.

Housing Development. Grant dollars for the development of affordable housing increased a modest 6 percent between 2002 and 2006, from $144.8 million to $153.5 million. By comparison, the number of grants

jumped 41 percent, close to three times the average growth for all social justice grants. By far, the organization receiving the most support in this area was Habitat for Humanity International (81 grants totaling $14.6 million). Among other grants captured in this area were a $500,000 award from the Meadows Foundation to the Housing Assistance Council to support a revolving loan fund to be used to construct affordable housing in rural areas of Texas; and a $250,000 grant from the Pittsburgh Foundation to the Pittsburgh Partnership for Neighborhood Development to develop affordable housing units in Pittsburgh.

Other. Most of the remaining housing and shelter funding in 2006 ($19.2 million) supported assistance to low-income families seeking home ownership, housing services, and activities advocating equal rights to housing. For example, the Fannie Mae Foundation awarded a $350,000 general support grant to the Mississippi-based Enterprise Corporation of the Delta for work to improve access to mortgage lending and home ownership for low- and moderate-income individuals in Arkansas, Louisiana, and Mississippi, and the Greater Memphis area of Tennessee.

> "Currently a program of the Wells Fargo Foundation, the Wells Fargo Housing Foundation's mission is to "provide sustainable homeownership opportunities for low-to moderate-income people by providing volunteer and financial resources to local and national nonprofit housing organizations."
>
> — Wells Fargo Foundation web site

Spotlight on Selected Grants

MARIN COMMUNITY FOUNDATION awarded $1.6 million to the California-based **Citizens Housing Corporation** for the Fireside Affordable Housing Project.

ABELL FOUNDATION awarded $200,000 to the **American Civil Liberties Union (ACLU) Foundation of Maryland** for continued support of the Regional Equity in Housing Project.

RETIREMENT RESEARCH FOUNDATION awarded $93,358 to the Illinois-based **John Marshall Law School** for research on housing discrimination against seniors.

Human Services

Human services captures only those social service grants that include the empowerment of vulnerable populations in their stated purpose. Grants that strictly provide services to vulnerable populations are excluded.

♦ **Support for social justice-related human services grew modestly from 2002 to 2006**

Human services captured 5.3 percent of social justice funding in 2006, down from 6.5 percent in 2002. Support for this area grew less than 7 percent during this period, far slower than overall social justice giving. Actual grant dollars rose from $114.4 million to $122.3 million. The number of grants grew even more slowly, from 1,218 grants in 2002 to 1,248 grants in 2006.

Top Funders

The Annie E. Casey Foundation provided by far the highest level of support for social justice-related human services in 2006 (Table 4-15). The foundation alone accounted for more than one-quarter of all funding, doubling its support from $15.2 million in 2002 to $31.4 million in 2006. One of Casey's larger grants in

this area was a $600,000 award to the DC-based Urban Institute to support Low-Income Working Families: Parents and Children Facing a World of Risk, a program of policy-relevant research and dissemination aimed at informing policy-makers about the fragile circumstances of low-income working families.

The next two largest funders were the W.K. Kellogg Foundation ($6.6 million) and the Ford Foundation ($5.4 million), which awarded 5.4 percent and 4.4 percent of funding, respectively. Ford's support included a $500,000 grant to the Los Angeles-based National Alliance of Latin American and Caribbean Communities. This grant funded projects to improve the quality of life for immigrant communities in the United States and in their countries of origin. Together, the top 10 foundations accounted for more than half (52.9 percent) of social justice-related human services giving.

TABLE 4-15 **Top 10 Human Services Funders, 2006**

Foundation Name	State	Grant Dollars	%	No. of Grants	%
1. Annie E. Casey Foundation	MD	$31,417,095	25.7	243	19.5
2. W.K. Kellogg Foundation	MI	6,555,111	5.4	28	2.2
3. Ford Foundation	NY	5,430,696	4.4	23	1.8
4. Houston Endowment	TX	4,845,000	4.0	3	0.2
5. John D. and Catherine T. MacArthur Foundation	IL	3,730,000	3.1	3	0.2
6. Marguerite Casey Foundation	WA	3,546,666	2.9	25	2.0
7. Citi Foundation	NY	2,834,500	2.3	52	4.2
8. Harry and Jeanette Weinberg Foundation	MD	2,285,000	1.9	11	0.9
9. California Wellness Foundation	CA	2,250,000	1.8	11	0.9
10. David and Lucile Packard Foundation	CA	1,795,000	1.5	8	0.6
Subtotal for Top 10		**$64,689,068**	**52.9**	**407**	**32.6**
Total		$122,258,944	100.0	1,248	100.0

Source: The Foundation Center, *Social Justice Grantmaking II*, 2009. Based on all grants of $10,000 or more awarded by a sample of 871 larger foundations.

Giving Trends

The majority of social justice-related human services funding ($90.1 million) supported multi-purpose social service programs targeting families, children, and youth.

For example, the Marguerite Casey Foundation awarded $250,000 to the Mexican American Legal Defense and Educational Fund (MALDEF) to expand its Parent Support and Leadership Programs and to more effectively coordinate the public policy and education at the state and national levels with its local parent leadership training programs. The balance of human services funding ranged from programs targeting nutrition and agriculture to financial counseling to public safety.

Spotlight on Selected Grants

FORD FOUNDATION awarded $500,000 to the Mississippi-based **Enterprise Corporation of the Delta** for financial counseling services and loan packaging to low-income homeowners in hurricane-affected areas of Mississippi.

W.K. KELLOGG FOUNDATION awarded $300,000 to the DC-based **Rural Coalition** to engage organizations serving farmers, farm workers, and rural communities of color in policy education and increase the capacity of these communities for leadership and advocacy.

STUART FOUNDATION awarded $75,000 to the Washington State-based **Children's Alliance** for a statewide network of child advocates working on issues that benefit Washington's children and families through implementation of public policies and programs, increased civic engagement and mobilization, and effective public information.

International Affairs, Peace, and Conflict Resolution

International affairs, peace, and conflict resolution includes support to ensure international peace and security, arms control, and conflict resolution. Funding also supports efforts focused on international trade and foreign policy.

♦ **International affairs funding grew by almost two-thirds between 2002 and 2006**

International affairs, peace, and conflict resolution accounted for 5 percent of social justice grant dollars in 2006, up from 4 percent in 2002. Funding rose by nearly two-thirds during this period—over twice the average for the social justice sample. Actual dollars climbed from $70 million to $115.8 million. At the same time, the number of international affairs grants showed a slight decline (down 3 percent).

Top Funders

Led by the John D. and Catherine T. MacArthur Foundation, the top 10 funders of international affairs, peace, and conflict resolution awarded more than three-quarters of the grant dollars in 2006 (Table 4-16). Among the 36 grants totaling almost $19 million awarded by MacArthur was a

$5 million operating grant to the Carnegie Endowment for International Peace. Overall, the Endowment received 18 social justice-related grants from foundations included in the 2006 sample.

Although the Ford Foundation continued to rank second based on social justice-related international affairs funding, its support decreased from $15.8 million to $14.2 million between 2002 and 2006. Ford's grants include a $1.2 million award to New York University's Center on International Cooperation for core support and for a project on strengthening multilateral approaches to nuclear and other weapons of mass destruction; and $400,000 to the PeaceWorks Foundation for core support for the One Voice Initiative to engage Israelis and Palestinians in a grassroots campaign for peace, including town hall meetings and youth leadership programs.

TABLE 4-16 **Top 10 International Affairs, Peace, and Conflict Resolution Funders, 2006**

Foundation Name	State	Grant Dollars	%	No. of Grants	%
1. John D. and Catherine T. MacArthur Foundation	IL	$18,979,231	16.4	36	6.9
2. Ford Foundation	NY	14,227,500	12.3	55	10.6
3. William and Flora Hewlett Foundation	CA	12,596,000	10.9	8	1.5
4. Bill & Melinda Gates Foundation	WA	10,400,000	9.0	2	0.4
5. Carnegie Corporation of New York	NY	9,980,500	8.6	41	7.9
6. Susan Thompson Buffett Foundation	NE	7,000,000	6.0	1	0.2
7. Peninsula Community Foundation	CA	6,079,600	5.3	19	3.7
8. Smith Richardson Foundation	CT	5,031,281	4.3	41	7.9
9. Ted Arison Charitable Trust	FL	3,750,000	3.2	1	0.2
10. Starr Foundation	NY	1,924,314	1.7	3	0.6
Subtotal for Top 10		**$89,968,426**	**77.7**	**207**	**39.9**
Total		$115,762,583	100.0	519	100.0

Source: The Foundation Center, *Social Justice Grantmaking II*, 2009. Based on all grants of $10,000 or more awarded by a sample of 871 larger foundations.

Giving Trends

Consistent with 2002 funding, the vast majority of grants in the 2006 sample targeting international affairs, peace, and conflict resolution supported peace and security, arms control, and conflict resolution. Examples include a $7 million award from the Susan Thompson Buffett Foundation to the Nuclear Threat Initiative for general support; and a $1 million grant from the Peninsula Community Foundation[7]

to the International Rescue Committee for Gender-Based Violence and Food Security for programs in the Darfur region of Sudan.

Additional funding was provided for trade and foreign policy efforts and public policy and research, including the the Bill & Melinda Gates Foundation's $10 million award to the DC-based Center for Global Development (CGD) to amplify the impact of CGD's policy research

and outreach on key public policy debates affecting health, education, governance, and economic outcomes in the developing world; and the Ford Foundation's $320,000 general support grant to the Coalition for Women's Economic Development and Global Equality, which engages in research and advocacy to influence U.S. international trade and investment policies to support sustainable livelihoods for poor women in developing countries.

Spotlight on Selected Grants

EXXONMOBIL FOUNDATION *awarded $100,000 to DC-based **Seeds of Peace** for the Conflict Management Program.*

SMITH RICHARDSON FOUNDATION *awarded $99,000 to the DC-based **American Foreign Policy Council** for Tolerant Islam in the War of Ideas Against Wahhabism, which examines how government and non-governmental leaders in Central Asia are countering Islamic radicalism.*

CARNEGIE CORPORATION OF NEW YORK *awarded $25,000 to the DC-based **Woodrow Wilson International Center for Scholars** for an international forum on the relationship between national security and civil liberties.*

Civic Engagement

Civic engagement captures efforts to engage diverse citizens in community affairs and public policy, increase citizen participation in government and democracy, and promote civic education and citizenship training in schools. It also encompasses support for grassroots leadership development and campaign finance and voter reform.

- ◆ Funding for civic engagement grew at a faster-than-average rate between 2002 and 2006
- ◆ Ford and Kellogg provided almost half of giving

Civic engagement accounted for 3.6 percent of social justice grant dollars in 2006, up slightly from 3.2 percent in 2002. Actual grant dollars increased 47 percent, from $56.3 million to $82.7 million, compared to 30.8 percent growth in social justice giving overall. The number of civic engagement grants increased just over 30 percent, or more than double the overall growth rate.

Top Funders

The Ford and W.K. Kellogg foundations accounted for close to half of giving (46.1 percent) for civic engagement in 2006 (Table 4-17). Ford led with $23.1 million in grant support, an increase of $4.4 million from 2002. However, this support

was provided through 75 grants in 2006, down from 113. The foundation awarded the largest grant for civic engagement in the latest year: $4 million to the DC-based Advocacy Institute for the Leadership for a Changing World Program to promote diverse models of leadership and to facilitate successful organizational leadership transition.

The second-ranked W.K. Kellogg Foundation increased its giving for civic engagement to $15 million in 2006, up from $1.8 million in 2002. This jump accounted for half of the increase in funding for the field. Among its awards was a $550,000 grant to Mozambique-based Fundacao Para o Desenvolvimento da Comunidade, Community Foundation Development Trust to strengthen the mechanisms for and the capacity of civil society organizations to participate in the development, monitoring, and evaluation of a national anti-poverty program.

FIGURE 4-13 **Civic Engagement, Giving to Subcategories, 2006**

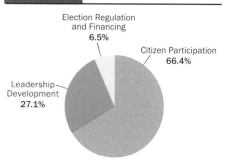

Election Regulation and Financing
6.5%

Citizen Participation
66.4%

Leadership Development
27.1%

Percent of Grant Dollars

Source: The Foundation Center, *Social Justice Grantmaking II*, 2009. Based on all grants of $10,000 or more awarded by a sample of 871 larger foundations.

TABLE 4-17 **Top 10 Civic Engagement Funders, 2006**

Foundation Name	State	Grant Dollars	%	No. of Grants	%
1. Ford Foundation	NY	$23,121,600	27.9	75	12.7
2. W.K. Kellogg Foundation	MI	15,016,941	18.2	25	4.2
3. Carnegie Corporation of New York	NY	5,167,800	6.2	37	6.3
4. Charles Stewart Mott Foundation	MI	3,203,235	3.9	35	5.9
5. Goldman Sachs Foundation	NY	2,865,000	3.5	1	0.2
6. Joyce Foundation	IL	2,236,250	2.7	8	1.4
7. Open Society Institute	NY	2,055,000	2.5	9	1.5
8. Rockefeller Brothers Fund	NY	1,919,000	2.3	16	2.7
9. JEHT Foundation[1]	NY	1,711,652	2.1	13	2.2
10. Andrew W. Mellon Foundation	NY	1,600,000	1.9	1	0.2
Subtotal for Top 10		**$58,896,478**	**71.2**	**220**	**37.3**
Total		$82,732,053	100.0	592	100.0

Source: The Foundation Center, *Social Justice Grantmaking II*, 2009. Based on all grants of $10,000 or more awarded by a sample of 871 larger foundations.
[1]The foundation ceased operation in January 2009.

Giving Trends

The majority of the funding for civic engagement supported organizations and programs working to increase participation in community affairs, government, and public policy by underrepresented and disenfranchised groups (Figure 4-13). The balance of support funded leadership development efforts and activities fostering campaign finance and voter reform.

Citizen Participation. Support for efforts to secure the inclusion of under-represented populations in the political and economic life of their communities commanded two-thirds of civic engagement dollars in 2006. Funding grew by more than one-third, from $40.2 million in 2002 to $54.9 million in 2006. Examples of grants in this area include a $225,000 award from the Bush Foundation to the Minnesota-based Center for Rural Policy and Development to establish a statewide rural civic engagement program; and a $120,000 general support grant from the Charles Stewart Mott Foundation to the Civic Initiative in Serbia.

Leadership Development. Support for efforts to develop the leadership skills of underrepresented and disenfranchised populations climbed more than three-fold between 2002 and 2006, while the number of grants rose a modest 5 percent. Among the 148 grants given in this area was an $880,675 award from the Freeman Foundation to the Honolulu-based Center for Cultural and Technical Interchange Between East and West, East West Center, for the Asia Pacific Leadership program; and a $125,000 grant from the AT&T Foundation to the Congressional Black Caucus Foundation for the Leadership Institute's national leadership development initiatives to educate African Americans about the importance of public policy and social responsibility.

Election Regulation and Financing. Support for election regulation, campaign finance reform, and voter education accounted for 6.5 percent of funding for civic engagement, down from 15.4 percent in 2002. Actual grant dollars dropped 38 percent during this period. Nonetheless, the

number of grants remained relatively stable. In 2006, the largest grant in this area was a $500,000 award from the James Irvine Foundation to the Los Angeles-based Center for Governmental Studies to develop and promote nonpartisan governance reforms on redistricting, the ballot initiative process, and the campaign finance system.

> "Ultimately, the Kellogg Foundation's goal is to strengthen communities by helping individuals who are already engaged in community stewardship to recognize themselves as leaders and join with others to develop the shared leadership expertise required to work across a range of backgrounds and perspectives."
>
> — W.K. Kellogg Foundation web site

Spotlight on Selected Grants

CARNEGIE CORPORATION OF NEW YORK awarded $1 million to New York-based **Public Interest Projects** for a funder collaborative on immigrant civic integration.

DUKE ENDOWMENT awarded $500,000 to North Carolina-based **Duke University** to expand its Baldwin Scholars Program, a four-year undergraduate women's leadership program.

COMMUNITY FOUNDATION FOR GREATER ATLANTA awarded $82,500 to the Georgia-based **Leadership Center at Morehouse College**, which trains new leaders to address contemporary ethical and social concerns, especially those affecting African–American life and culture.

Crime and Justice

C rime and justice encompasses support for legal services aimed at assisting low-income individuals and other vulnerable populations and public interest litigation addressing a range of social justice issues. It also includes support for criminal justice reform and for various other activities, such as juvenile and domestic violence prevention and ensuring the rights of offenders and ex-offenders.

◆ Support for crime and justice grew by over one-third between 2002 and 2006

◆ MacArthur Foundation and Open Society Institute provided largest shares of funding

Crime and justice represented 3.5 percent of social justice grantmaking in 2006, up slightly from 2002, while actual grant dollars rose by almost 38 percent to $81.3 million. By comparison, the share of number of grants climbed from 5.3 percent to 6.2 percent during this period. Overall, the median grant amount for crime and justice was $35,000, compared to $45,000 for all social justice grants in 2006.

Top Funders

The John D. and Catherine T. MacArthur Foundation and the Open Society Institute (OSI) accounted for close to one-third (31.4 percent) of crime and justice giving in 2006 (Table 4-18). MacArthur awarded

$13.4 million in this category, up $10.4 million from 2002. Contributing to this increase was MacArthur's support for the reform of the juvenile justice system in the United States, including a $1.5 million grant to the Center for Children's Law and Policy for activities to reduce the disproportionate minority contact and racial and ethnic disparities in the juvenile justice systems in states where Models for Change efforts are taking place. The Models for Change initiative seeks to create successful and replicable models of juvenile justice system reform.

Second-ranked OSI provided $12.1 million for efforts related to crime and justice and, in fact, awarded the largest number of grants (72) in this area. The foundation's two largest grants in 2006 totaled $1.9 million and supported fellowships for Equal Justice Works, an organization that provides training and skills to enable attorneys to provide effective representation to vulnerable populations.

FIGURE 4-14 **Crime and Justice, Giving to Subcategories, 2006**

- Legal Services 45.3%
- Other 28.1%
- Administration of Justice/Courts 26.6%

Percent of Grant Dollars

Source: The Foundation Center, *Social Justice Grantmaking II*, 2009. Based on all grants of $10,000 or more awarded by a sample of 871 larger foundations.

TABLE 4-18 **Top 10 Crime and Justice Funders, 2006**

Foundation Name	State	Grant Dollars	%	No. of Grants	%
1. John D. and Catherine T. MacArthur Foundation	IL	$13,437,600	16.5	30	3.2
2. Open Society Institute	NY	12,118,894	14.9	72	7.7
3. Robert Wood Johnson Foundation	NJ	6,000,000	7.4	1	0.1
4. Ford Foundation	NY	5,287,705	6.5	30	3.2
5. JEHT Foundation[1]	NY	4,779,156	5.9	32	3.4
6. Annie E. Casey Foundation	MD	4,313,459	5.3	47	5.0
7. New York Community Trust	NY	2,801,300	3.4	51	5.4
8. California Endowment	CA	1,619,810	2.0	8	0.9
9. Public Welfare Foundation	DC	1,508,000	1.9	29	3.1
10. Otto Bremer Foundation	MN	640,852	0.8	20	2.1
Subtotal for Top 10		**$52,506,776**	**64.6**	**320**	**34.1**
Total		$81,256,506	100.0	938	100.0

Source: The Foundation Center, *Social Justice Grantmaking II*, 2009. Based on all grants of $10,000 or more awarded by a sample of 871 larger foundations.
[1] The foundation ceased operation in January 2009.

Giving Trends

Close to half of crime and justice funding supported legal services for low-income and underrepresented populations (Figure 4-14). The balance of funding was roughly equally divided between support for issues related to reforming the judicial system and grantmaking in support of activities such as ensuring the rights of offenders and ex-offenders, abuse and crime prevention, and law enforcement reform. The vast majority of grants supported programs based in the United States.

Legal Services. Support for providers of legal assistance to vulnerable populations and for public interest litigation rose by nearly 12 percent between 2002 and 2006, reaching $36.8 million. In contrast, the number of grants grew by 43.4 percent, close to three times the average for the social justice sample overall. Funding in this area included a $416,667 grant from the JEHT Foundation[8] to the Innocence Project, a national litigation and public policy organization dedicated to exonerating wrongfully convicted people through DNA testing and reforming the criminal justice

system to prevent future injustice; and a $120,000 grant from the Nina Mason Pulliam Charitable Trust to the Neighborhood Christian Legal Clinic for the Immigrants in Crisis Project, which assists new immigrants who are victims of human trafficking, violent crime, and/or domestic violence.

Administration of Justice/Courts. Funding to support and reform the judicial system, including a strong focus on juvenile justice reform, increased by more than four-fifths between 2002 and 2006 and reached $21.6 million. The John D. and Catherine T. MacArthur Foundation awarded the top five grants in this area, including a $675,000 grant to the DC-based Justice Policy Institute for policy, advocacy, and communications planning for the previously noted Models for Change initiative. A more modest example of funding in this area was the Wallace Global Fund's $50,000 grant to the Families Against Mandatory Minimums Foundation for general support of its work to reform harsh mandatory sentencing laws at the federal and state level.

Other. Most of the remaining crime and justice grant dollars focused

> "Developing an international system of justice, strengthening human rights protections in countries in transition abroad, and reforming our juvenile justice system at home are the three pillars of MacArthur's commitment to advancing justice."
>
> — John D. and Catherine T. MacArthur Foundation Annual Report

on programs for offenders and ex-offenders, including those that work to ensure their rights. Support also included activities ranging from abuse, delinquency, and crime prevention to law enforcement reform. Together, funding in these areas increased by almost two-thirds to $22.9 million in 2006. Support included the William Randolph Hearst Foundation's $75,000 grant to Miami-based Voices for Children Foundation to provide support services and representation for abused and neglected children.

Spotlight on Selected Grants

FORD FOUNDATION awarded $220,000 to the **Ohio Justice and Policy Center** to establish the Race and Criminal Justice Project, which will undertake public education and litigation to reduce overrepresentation of racial and ethnic minorities in the criminal justice system.

SURDNA FOUNDATION awarded $100,000 to the California-based **Ella Baker Center for Human Rights** for the Books Not Bars Alternatives for Youth Campaign, an effort to win comprehensive reforms of California's juvenile justice system.

ANNIE E. CASEY FOUNDATION awarded $10,000 to the **Public Interest Law Center of Philadelphia** to investigate economic and legal barriers faced by individuals leaving prison and attempting to resume their lives as productive citizens in their communities.

Environment and Environmental Justice

Environment and environmental justice includes efforts to develop environmentally sustainable communities and secure environmental justice for vulnerable communities in the United States and around the world.

- ◆ The environment maintained a consistent share of support between 2002 and 2006

- ◆ Almost half of the funding supported international activities

Environment and environmental justice accounted for 1.9 percent of social justice dollars in 2006, matching its 2002 share. Actual grant dollars grew from $33 million to $43.4 million. By comparison, the number of awards rose a marginal 1.6 percent, from 376 to 382.

Top Funders

The Ford Foundation ranked as the largest funder for the environment and environmental justice in 2006 (Table 4-19), providing close to one-quarter of the dollars ($9.9 million) and far surpassing the second-ranked Gordon and Betty Moore Foundation ($3.9 million). Nonetheless, Ford's giving in this area was down $6.8 million from $16.7 million in 2002. Its support in the latest year

included a $300,000 grant to the California-based National Community Development Institute to provide training and consulting services to emerging environmental justice leaders. Among the eight grants awarded by the Moore Foundation was a $837,945 award for Centro de Trabalho Indigenista to create and improve management of indigenous territories for isolated Indians in Southwestern Brazil.

Giving Trends

Environmental funding supported work on public policy, advocacy, research, development, and legal rights related to conservation and environmental protection. Almost half of this support (47.5 percent) targeted international programs based in the United States or recipients in other countries. Internationally focused environmental grants included the W.K. Kellogg Foundation's $100,000 award to the Mexico-based United Nations Environment Programme to

TABLE 4-19 **Top 10 Environment and Environmental Justice Funders, 2006**

Foundation Name	State	Grant Dollars	%	No. of Grants	%
1. Ford Foundation	NY	$9,920,375	22.8	55	14.4
2. Gordon and Betty Moore Foundation	CA	3,929,702	9.0	8	2.1
3. Bill & Melinda Gates Foundation	WA	3,300,000	7.6	1	0.3
4. Charles Stewart Mott Foundation	MI	2,460,461	5.7	17	4.5
5. William and Flora Hewlett Foundation	CA	2,020,000	4.6	15	3.9
6. John D. and Catherine T. MacArthur Foundation	IL	1,785,000	4.1	9	2.4
7. California Endowment	CA	1,513,339	3.5	7	1.8
8. W.K. Kellogg Foundation	MI	1,495,000	3.4	5	1.3
9. Richard and Rhoda Goldman Fund	CA	1,255,000	2.9	10	2.6
10. James Irvine Foundation	CA	1,100,000	2.5	5	1.3
Subtotal for Top 10		**$28,778,877**	**66.1**	**132**	**34.6**
Total		$43,442,417	100.0	382	100.0

Source: The Foundation Center, *Social Justice Grantmaking II*, 2009. Based on all grants of $10,000 or more awarded by a sample of 871 larger foundations.

enhance environmental awareness and the participation of civil society and nongovernmental organizations in rural areas and deprived urban areas of Central America and the Caribbean by developing a training course for journalists, women, and youth leaders.

Domestic grants included a $50,000 award from the Beldon Fund to the New Mexico-based SouthWest Organizing Project for efforts to train youth in disenfranchised communities in the Southwest to be environmental justice advocates and leaders.

"We work to support natural resource management and environmental justice strategies that help poor communities overcome environment and development challenges, as well as the economic exclusion and social marginalization that underlie them."

— Ford Foundation web site

Spotlight on Selected Grants

FORD FOUNDATION awarded $200,000 to California-based Pacific Environment for technical assistance to the Sosnovka Coalition of NGOs working in the fields of sustainable environmental management and environmental justice in Siberia and the Russian Far East.

FUND FOR NEW JERSEY awarded $60,000 to the New Jersey-based Clean Water Fund for renewed support for statewide and urban environmental justice work to protect those most vulnerable to harmful substances at home, school, work, and in the community.

JESSIE SMITH NOYES FOUNDATION awarded $20,000 in general support to New York-based Families United for Racial and Economic Equality for grassroots organizing and to build the collective power of low-income families and people of color in Brooklyn to make systemic changes for a more environmentally just and socially sustainable New York.

Employment Development and Rights

Employment development and rights encompasses support for efforts to increase workforce participation, skill levels, and compensation among vulnerable populations and to promote equality in employment.

♦ **Giving for employment development and rights was nearly unchanged between 2002 and 2006**

♦ **Ford Foundation provided almost one-quarter of funding**

Funding for employment development and rights accounted for 1.9 percent of social justice funding in 2006, down from 2.4 percent in 2002. Despite increased giving by a few major foundations, overall grant dollars remained virtually flat at $42.7 million, and the number of grants declined slightly.

Top Funders

The Ford Foundation ranked as the largest funder for employment development and rights in 2006. It provided $10.2 million for this area in the latest year—or nearly one-quarter of giving—up from $6.4 million in 2002 (Table 4-20). Ford's support included a $400,000 grant to DC-based Jobs with Justice for

general support to create and sustain long-term, multi-issue coalitions for economic justice and to build a national network of these coalitions.

In addition to Ford, the Joyce Foundation was the only funder ranked among the top 10 supporters of employment development and rights in both 2002 and 2006 to increase giving for this area. Grantmakers new to the list of top 10 funders in the latest year included the Marguerite Casey, Public Welfare, Alfred P. Sloan, and John S. and James L. Knight foundations.

Giving Trends

The vast majority of funding in the employment development and rights area supported employment services and training programs for low-income and vulnerable populations. For example, the Joyce Foundation awarded the largest grant in this area—$2.4 million to New York City-based MDRC, to conduct a

| TABLE 4-20 | Top 10 Employment Development and Rights Funders, 2006 |

Foundation Name	State	Grant Dollars	%	No. of Grants	%
1. Ford Foundation	NY	$10,247,740	24.0	36	9.4
2. Joyce Foundation	IL	6,169,760	14.5	14	3.7
3. Charles Stewart Mott Foundation	MI	3,279,228	7.7	18	4.7
4. Marguerite Casey Foundation	WA	2,599,166	6.1	10	2.6
5. Annie E. Casey Foundation	MD	2,058,650	4.8	24	6.3
6. Rockefeller Foundation	NY	1,800,000	4.2	4	1.0
7. Public Welfare Foundation	DC	1,360,000	3.2	28	7.3
8. Alfred P. Sloan Foundation	NY	1,358,382	3.2	6	1.6
9. John S. and James L. Knight Foundation	FL	1,000,000	2.3	1	0.3
10. Rosenberg Foundation	CA	862,000	2.0	8	2.1
Subtotal for Top 10		**$30,734,926**	**72.0**	**149**	**39.0**
Total		$42,680,791	100.0	383	100.0

Source: The Foundation Center, *Social Justice Grantmaking II*, 2009. Based on all grants of $10,000 or more awarded by a sample of 871 larger foundations.

multi-component evaluation of transitional jobs programs serving male ex-offenders.

Funders also supported efforts to secure equal rights and inform public policy on employment-related issues, such as the California Wellness Foundation's $150,000 grant to the University of California at San Diego for the San Diego Regional Consortium to continue to evaluate components of the pipeline program intended to increase diversity in health professions.

"Why Workers' Rights? Because one in eight people in this country lives below the poverty line. Millions more struggle to pay for basic necessities. And low-wage jobs are the type of jobs that are least likely to provide employer based benefits."

— Public Welfare Foundation Annual Report

Spotlight on Selected Grants

ROSENBERG FOUNDATION awarded $100,000 to California-based **Sweatshop Watch** for a Garment Worker Center in Oakland.

ROCKEFELLER FOUNDATION awarded $300,000 in general support to the DC-based **Jobs with Justice Education Fund** to provide technical assistance to local coalitions that connect labor, faith-based, community, and student organizations to engage working people in taking action to improve their quality of life through workplace democracy and civic participation.

MEYER MEMORIAL TRUST awarded $125,000 to the Oregon-based **Northwest Employment Education and Defense Fund** for continued support for legal and educational services to low-wage workers.

Public Affairs

Public affairs encompasses support for efforts to promote the effective functioning of government and government programs that will result in improvements in government responsiveness to disadvantaged populations.

- ◆ **Support for public affairs declined between 2002 and 2006**
- ◆ **Ford and Gates provided more than one-third of grant dollars**

Funding for public affairs represented 1.8 percent of social justice-related grant dollars in 2006, down from 2.9 percent in 2002. Actual grant dollars fell almost 16 percent—from $50.5 million to $42.6 million. Public affairs was one of three areas of social justice funding that experienced decreases in giving in the latest year. The number of grants also fell 9.3 percent, from 365 to 331.

Top Funders

The Ford Foundation and the Bill & Melinda Gates Foundation dominated giving for public affairs in 2006 (Table 4-21). Together, these foundations awarded more than one-third (35.5 percent) of grant dollars. Among Ford's 19 grants in this area was a $600,000 award to United for a Fair Economy to strengthen the capacity of grassroots groups to understand and participate in the growing national conversation about tax and budget policy and the particular impact on communities of color. The second-ranked Gates Foundation was new to the top 10 public affairs funders in 2006, awarding $7.4 million—almost equal to Ford's $7.7 million. Gates provided four grants, including the largest for public affairs—$6 million to the Maryland-based University Research Corporation International to assess the impact of grants made to develop innovative financial services for the poor.

Giving Trends

The vast majority of 2006 public affairs support targeted government financing and administration (Figure 4-15), and support increased dramatically compared to 2002. In contrast, funding for welfare policy and reform and multipurpose policy and reform experienced steep declines during this period.

FIGURE 4-15 | **Public Affairs, Giving to Subcategories, 2006**

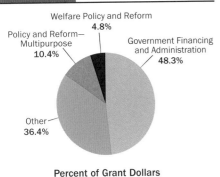

Welfare Policy and Reform 4.8%
Policy and Reform—Multipurpose 10.4%
Government Financing and Administration 48.3%
Other 36.4%

Percent of Grant Dollars

Source: The Foundation Center, *Social Justice Grantmaking II*, 2009. Based on all grants of $10,000 or more awarded by a sample of 871 larger foundations.

TABLE 4-21 | **Top 10 Public Affairs Funders, 2006**

Foundation Name	State	Grant Dollars	%	No. of Grants	%
1. Ford Foundation	NY	$7,723,000	18.1	19	5.7
2. Bill & Melinda Gates Foundation	WA	7,415,773	17.4	4	1.2
3. Annie E. Casey Foundation	MD	4,819,496	11.3	62	18.7
4. John D. and Catherine T. MacArthur Foundation	IL	2,300,000	5.4	4	1.2
5. Charles Stewart Mott Foundation	MI	1,881,000	4.4	16	4.8
6. Rockefeller Foundation	NY	1,550,000	3.6	3	0.9
7. AT&T Foundation	TX	1,488,584	3.5	3	0.9
8. Marguerite Casey Foundation	WA	1,435,000	3.4	4	1.2
9. Open Society Institute	NY	990,000	2.3	11	3.3
10. Lannan Foundation	NM	710,000	1.7	4	1.2
Subtotal for Top 10		**$30,312,853**	**71.1**	**130**	**39.1**
Total		$42,552,952	100	331	100

Source: The Foundation Center, *Social Justice Grantmaking II*, 2009. Based on all grants of $10,000 or more awarded by a sample of 871 larger foundations.

Government Financing and Administration. Grantmaking focused on government financing and administration that affects disadvantaged populations commanded almost half (48.3 percent) of public affairs giving in 2006, and dollars more than doubled from $8.7 million in 2002 to $20.6 million.

The DC-based Center on Budget and Policy Priorities received 24 grants in this area, including a $1 million award from the Ford Foundation to analyze the impact of U.S. fiscal and social policies on low-income populations.

Policy and Reform—Multipurpose. Funding for policy and reform activities, which primarily address economic and social policy research, decreased by almost two-thirds between 2002 and 2006. Grant dollars totaled $4.4 million in the latest year, down from $11.8 million. Among the 62 grants in this area was a $100,000 award from the Lynde and Harry Bradley Foundation to Texas A & M University for research on Social Security and Medicare reform.

Welfare Policy and Reform. Support for policy analysis, advocacy efforts, and public education on government welfare policy decreased dramatically between 2002 and 2006. Actual grant dollars dropped nearly 89 percent, from $18.5 million to $2.1 million, while the number of grants declined from 102 to 23. Among funders still active in this area was the Charles Stewart Mott Foundation, whose support included a $70,000 grant to the Center for Law and Social Policy to provide technical assistance for the Leading Edge States Project, which will help state policymakers, administrators, and program providers interpret and implement a new federal welfare reform law to improve the economic well-being of low-income families and their children.

> "We fund projects to identify and promote promising safety net reforms; protect and strengthen the federal and state revenues that finance such programs; and ensure that low- and moderate-income families have opportunities and incentives to build assets."
>
> — Charles Stewart Mott Foundation web site

Spotlight on Selected Grants

JOYCE FOUNDATION awarded $400,000 to the DC-based Center on Budget and Policy Priorities for national budget and policy analyses related to low-income workers and for technical assistance to state-level advocates in the Midwest.

FORD FOUNDATION awarded $250,000 to the New York-based Levy Economics Institute at Bard College to conduct comparative research on the gender dimensions of taxation and tax policy reforms in the context of globalization and disseminate findings.

AT&T FOUNDATION awarded $35,000 to the DC-based Alliance for Public Technology for an educational initiative designed to inform nonprofit leaders about the impact of telecom policies for their constituencies and what can be done to ensure the best interests of the diverse populations they serve.

Arts, Culture, and Media

Arts, culture, and media captures efforts to increase the participation of underserved and minority populations in media and journalism, the humanities, and the arts and to expand cultural and ethnic awareness.

◆ **Support for social justice-related arts, culture, and media more than doubled between 2002 and 2006**

◆ **Wallace Foundation provided almost one-quarter of support**

Support for arts, culture, and media more than doubled between 2002 and 2006, from $18.1 million to $36.4 million. As a result, arts-related social justice giving reached 1.6 percent of grant dollars, up from 1 percent in 2002. By comparsion, the share of number of grants remained unchanged at 1.6 percent.

Top Funders

The dramatic growth in arts-related social justice funding was largely due to increased giving by the Wallace Foundation—the top-ranked funder in this area in 2006. The foundation accounted for almost one-quarter of grants dollars and 46 percent of the increase in funding between 2002 and 2006 (Table 4-22). It also provided the largest grant reported in the latest year: an $8 million award to Dallas-based Big Thought for the Dallas Arts Learning Initiative, a program that will raise the quality of and access to arts learning for all Dallas youth in and out of school by coordinating and strengthening providers, communicating opportunities, and reducing barriers.

The Ford Foundation ranked second, giving $5.9 million in 2006, up from $4.9 million in 2002. Its support for arts-related social justice activities included a $1.1 million grant to the New York City-based International Coalition of Historic Site Museums of Conscience to build institutional capacity, identify new leadership, develop a strategic plan, and help members preserve sites of struggles for human rights and democracy around world. Together, the top 10 funders in this area provided almost three-quarters of grant dollars.

TABLE 4-22 **Top 10 Arts, Culture, and Media Funders, 2006**

Foundation Name	State	Grant Dollars	%	No. of Grants	%
1. Wallace Foundation	NY	$8,400,000	23.1	2	0.8
2. Ford Foundation	NY	5,866,200	16.1	23	9.2
3. Walt Disney Company Foundation	CA	2,500,000	6.9	1	0.4
4. Freedom Forum	VA	2,325,485	6.4	2	0.8
5. Greenspun Family Foundation	NV	2,000,000	5.5	1	0.4
6. General Motors Foundation	MI	1,510,000	4.2	2	0.8
7. James Irvine Foundation	CA	1,295,000	3.6	4	1.6
8. Annenberg Foundation	PA	1,125,000	3.1	2	0.8
9. ExxonMobil Foundation	TX	1,000,000	2.7	1	0.4
10. John S. and James L. Knight Foundation	FL	750,000	2.1	1	0.4
Subtotal for Top 10		**$26,771,685**	**73.6**	**39**	**15.5**
Total		$36,365,580	100.0	251	100.0

Source: The Foundation Center, *Social Justice Grantmaking II*, 2009. Based on all grants of $10,000 or more awarded by a sample of 871 larger foundations.

Giving Trends

Within social justice-related arts, culture, and media, the largest shares of funding supported efforts to increase minority participation in performing arts education, journalism, and other media, social justice-related memorials and museums, and programs fostering cultural and ethnic awareness. Among these awards was the Freedom Forum's $2.3 million grant to Vanderbilt University for the Freedom Forum Diversity Institute, which trains mid-career people of color for professional positions in daily newspaper newsrooms; and the Walt Disney Company Foundation's $2.5 million award to the Washington, DC-based Martin Luther King, Jr. National Memorial Project Foundation.

Spotlight on Selected Grants

JOHN S. AND JAMES L. KNIGHT FOUNDATION awarded $750,000 to Indiana-based **Arts United of Greater Fort Wayne** to help the city embrace new residents by increasing the community's understanding and appreciation of other cultures through a process that strengthens the development of arts organizations in culturally diverse, underserved communities in Fort Wayne.

WILLIAM AND FLORA HEWLETT FOUNDATION awarded $250,000 to the California-based **Destiny Arts Center** for dance, theater, martial arts, violence prevention, and leadership instruction to young people as a means to end isolation, prejudice, and violence in Richmond.

W.K. KELLOGG FOUNDATION awarded $75,000 to the North Carolina-based **Southern Rural Development Initiative** to enable teams of young cultural workers from across the South to use a range of art forms to honor exceptional and diverse people who have helped make rural communities more just and sustainable.

Social Science Research

Social science research includes social justice-related activities spanning the social science disciplines, including disciplines such as international and peace studies, law and international law, population and poverty studies, ethnic and women's studies, economic and labor studies, and social science interdisciplinary studies.

◆ **Funding for social science research experienced the fastest decline in funding between 2002 and 2006**

◆ **Close to two-thirds of support targeted international activities**

Social science research received 1.5 percent of social justice grant dollars in 2006, down from 3.3 percent in 2002. Actual grant dollars decreased by just over 40 percent to $34.3 million. The number of grants also decreased 21 percent. The reduction in giving for social science research was the steepest among the three social justice fields reporting reduced support.

The vast majority of social science research grant dollars (62.1 percent) funded international projects in the United States or overseas recipients. By comparison, a far smaller 39.5 percent of overall social justice grant dollars supported international activities in 2006.

Top Funders

Led by the Ford Foundation, the top 10 funders provided nearly three-quarters of grant dollars for social science research in 2006 (Table 4-23). Ford alone accounted for one-quarter of the funding, although its giving decreased by $5.8 million between 2002 and 2006. Compounding the reduction in Ford's giving was the loss of the Lilly Endowment and the Andrew Mellon Foundation among the top 10 funders. In 2002, they ranked second and third. The largest social science research grant reported in the latest year was the Starr Foundation's $5 million award to Friends of the Central and East European Law Initiative Institute for renovations to the main Institute building. The organization serves as a catalyst for reform in legal, judicial, and parliamentary education throughout Central and Eastern Europe and the former Soviet Union.

TABLE 4-23 **Top 10 Social Science Research Funders, 2006**

Foundation Name	State	Grant Dollars	%	No. of Grants	%
1. Ford Foundation	NY	$8,610,845	25.1	55	27.6
2. Starr Foundation	NY	5,150,000	15.0	2	1.0
3. Carnegie Corporation of New York	NY	3,250,100	9.5	7	3.5
4. Annie E. Casey Foundation	MD	1,970,345	5.8	10	5.0
5. Charles Stewart Mott Foundation	MI	1,500,623	4.4	9	4.5
6. John D. and Catherine T. MacArthur Foundation	IL	1,477,181	4.3	9	4.5
7. Smith Richardson Foundation	CT	1,244,809	3.6	11	5.5
8. Spencer Foundation	IL	798,975	2.3	3	1.5
9. David and Lucile Packard Foundation	CA	730,000	2.1	4	2.0
10. William and Flora Hewlett Foundation	CA	700,000	2.0	3	1.5
Subtotal for Top 10		**$25,432,878**	**74.1**	**113**	**56.6**
Total		$34,253,339	100.0	199	100.0

Source: The Foundation Center, *Social Justice Grantmaking II*, 2009. Based on all grants of $10,000 or more awarded by a sample of 871 larger foundations.

Giving Trends

The largest share of giving for social science research in 2006 targeted law and international law studies and research, and international studies.

In addition to the Starr Foundation grant noted above, the Henry Luce Foundation, for example, awarded $480,000 to Emory University for development of the Program on Law, Religion, and Human Rights.

The next two largest areas of giving were for poverty and social science interdisciplinary studies, followed by economic, population, labor, ethnic, rural, and women's studies.

Spotlight on Selected Grants

HOWARD G. BUFFETT FOUNDATION awarded $174,000 to Georgia-based **CARE** for a program assessing the social and economic costs of protected areas on poverty in Uganda, Kenya, Thailand, and the Philippines.

ROCKEFELLER FOUNDATION awarded $125,000 to the **Center for Latin American Studies at the University of California at Berkeley** for the U.S.-Mexico Future's Forum, which provides opportunities for dialogue among scholars, policymakers, community and union leaders, journalists, and business groups on migration and the integration of migrants into U.S. society.

THE CHRISTENSEN FUND awarded $60,000 to the Australia-based **University of Queensland** for the establishment of the International Journal of Critical Race and Whiteness Studies and publication and distribution of its first four hard-copy issues to advance understanding of the causes and consequences of racism.

Social Justice Funding by Population Groups

The Foundation Center's grants classification system includes 21 major beneficiary groups. Grants are coded for specific population groups whenever the intended beneficiary is noted in the grant description or when the beneficiary is clear from the name and purpose of the recipient organization. If more than one population group—e.g., economically disadvantaged youth—is the intended beneficiary of a grant, the grant is added to the total amount reported for each applicable category. Because grants may be counted more than once, each category is analyzed as a percentage of the total grant dollars and number of grants reported.

♦ Most social justice grants targeted specific population groups

♦ Economically disadvantaged were targeted in the majority of social justice grants

The vast majority of social justice grants (84.2 percent) were coded as benefiting one or more population groups. This comes as no surprise given the role of social justice funding in addressing social inequities (Table 4-24).[9] By comparison, less than half (46.9 percent) of grants in the Foundation Center's overall sample were coded for specific population groups

In the 2006 social justice sample, the economically disadvantaged benefited from by far the largest share of social justice support—63.9 percent of grant dollars and 59.5 percent of grants. Ethnic or racial minorities followed with almost one-quarter of grant

dollars and close to one-third of the grants. Only two other population groups were targeted with at least 10 percent of social justice grant dollars in the latest sample—children and youth (17.9 percent) and women and girls (11.4 percent).

Growth patterns from 2002 to 2006 varied considerably among population groups (Figure 4-16). The economically disadvantaged experienced above-average growth in both social justice-related grant dollars (up 47.1 percent) and number of grants (up 24.1 percent), while ethnic and racial minorities showed below-average growth—up 7.8 percent by grant dollars and 11.1 percent by number of grants. There were also pronounced variations in growth among the specified ethnic and racial minority groups. Funding for Native Americans and Hispanics and Latinos

FIGURE 4-16 Change in Social Justice Giving by Population Group, 2002 and 2006

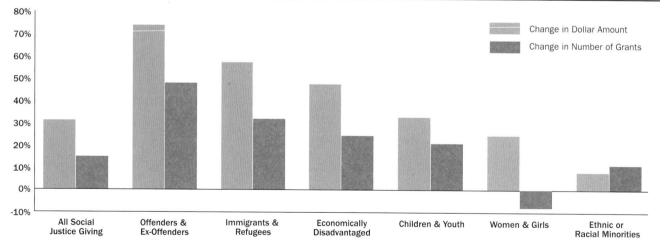

Source: The Foundation Center, *Social Justice Grantmaking II*, 2009. Based on all grants of $10,000 or more awarded by a sample of 749 larger foundations for 2002 and 871 for 2006. Includes population groups accounting for more that 2 percent of grant dollars.

grew between 2002 and 2006—up 62.2 percent and 21.3 percent, respectively—while funding for African Americans and Blacks and for Asians and Pacific Islanders declined—down 18.9 percent and 26.9 percent, respectively. Five other population groups experienced above-average growth in grant dollars during this period, including gays and lesbians (up 115 percent), people with AIDS (up 110.4 percent), offenders and ex-offenders (up 73.4 percent), immigrants and refugees (up 56.8 percent), and men and boys (up 40.9 percent).

TABLE 4-24	Social Justice Giving by Population Group, 2006			
Group	Amount	%	No. of Grants	%
Aging/Elderly/Senior Citizens	$40,930,587	1.8	425	2.8
Children & Youth	411,177,485	17.9	2,662	17.4
Crime or Abuse Victims	27,273,578	1.2	343	2.2
Economically Disadvantaged	1,469,647,262	63.9	9,088	59.5
Poor, Indigent—General	1,419,354,371	61.7	8,627	56.4
Homeless	40,593,528	1.8	360	2.4
Migrant Workers	9,699,363	0.4	101	0.7
Ethnic or Racial Minorities[1]	572,129,089	24.8	4,662	30.5
General	301,369,451	13.1	2,507	16.4
Asians & Pacific Islanders	20,898,575	0.9	277	1.8
African Americans & Blacks	88,151,677	3.8	579	3.8
Hispanics & Latinos	81,910,848	3.6	748	4.9
Native Americans	49,121,135	2.1	238	1.6
Indigenous Peoples	14,936,056	0.6	122	0.8
Other Minorities	15,741,347	0.7	191	1.2
Gays or Lesbians	26,348,980	1.1	383	2.5
Immigrants & Refugees	131,595,505	5.7	1,112	7.3
Men & Boys	22,004,531	1.0	110	0.7
Military & Veterans	4,286,626	0.2	39	0.3
Offenders & Ex-Offenders	60,294,484	2.6	431	2.8
People with AIDS	21,186,838	0.9	166	1.1
People with Disabilities	40,787,929	1.8	516	3.4
People with Terminal Illness	1,586,419	0.1	21	0.1
Single Parents	1,158,500	0.1	23	0.2
Substance Abusers	8,629,042	0.4	89	0.6
Women & Girls	261,304,434	11.4	1,743	11.4
Not Specified/General Public	364,388,851	15.8	2,287	14.9

Source: The Foundation Center, *Social Justice Grantmaking II*, 2009. Based on all grants of $10,000 or more awarded by a sample of 871 larger foundations. Grants may benefit multiple population groups, e.g., a grant for homeless women and their children, and therefore figures are only representative.
[1]Coding for these groups generally includes only domestic populations. Overseas grants are only coded for ethnic or racial minorities if they specifically mention a benefit for a particular minority group.

SOCIAL JUSTICE GRANTMAKING FOR RURAL POPULATIONS

Social justice funders provided $180.2 million in grants specifically benefiting rural populations in 2006, up by nearly 79 percent from 2002. The number of social justice grants targeting rural populations also grew at an above-average rate during this period (25 percent versus 14.6 percent) and climbed from 519 to 649 grants.

Economic development efforts accounted for nearly half (49 percent) of social justice funding specifically focused on rural areas in 2006, including support for international agricultural development. Among the largest awards in this area was the Bill & Melinda Gates Foundation's $15 million grant to the Bangladesh Rural Advance Commission (BRAC), one of the world's largest nongovernmental development organizations. Access to health care ranked second, and

funding included a $25.2 million Gates grant to BRAC for support of access to reproductive health care. Together, these grants accounted for half of the increase in giving targeted to rural populations between 2002 and 2006.

Despite the impact of very large awards, relatively smaller social justice grants played a significant role in funding intended to benefit rural populations. In fact, more than two-thirds of rural-focused social justice awards were for $100,000 or less. An example of these grants was the Retirement Research Foundation's $100,000 award to the Des Moines-based Iowa Citizens for Community Improvement for the Rural Seniors Environmental Health and Justice Project.

Recipients of Social Justice Funding

A preceding section examined foundations' social justice grantmaking by subject areas funded. This section documents the types of organizations supported by these grants.[10]

♦ **Domestic-focused economic and community development organizations captured the largest share of social justice funding**

♦ **Support for international organizations and human service agencies posted the fastest growth between 2002 and 2006**

In 2006, a total of 6,955 organizations received social justice-related grants, up by 5 percent from 6,625 in 2002 (Table 4-2). However, the actual number of recipients benefiting from this support is likely to be far higher since some of these organizations serve as funding intermediaries, redistributing funds to the other organizations.

Among the various types of recipients receiving social justice support in 2006, domestically focused economic and community development organizations captured the largest share of funding—16.5 percent of

grant dollars and close to 18 percent of the number of grants (Table 4-25). New York City-based Local Initiatives Support Corporation (LISC) ranked as the largest economic and community development recipient, with 58 grants totaling $14.5 million.

Funding for international organizations matched economic and community development by share of grant dollars (16.5 percent), but these organizations benefited from a much smaller share of grants (9.6 percent). This category includes international economic development organizations, which accounted for more than two-fifths of funding in 2006. Taken together, support for international economic development organizations ($161.7 million) and domestic-focused economic and community development organizations ($380.4 million) totaled $542.1 million.

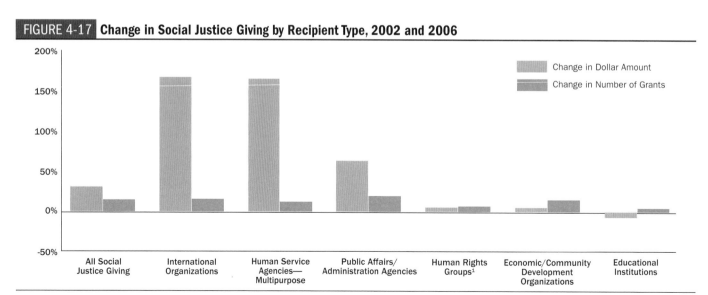

FIGURE 4-17 | **Change in Social Justice Giving by Recipient Type, 2002 and 2006**

Source: The Foundation Center, *Social Justice Grantmaking II*, 2009. Based on all grants of $10,000 or more awarded by a sample of 749 larger foundations for 2002 and 871 for 2006. Includes recipient types accounting for at least 8 percent of grant dollars in 2006.
[1]"Human Rights Groups" includes only domestic organizations; international human rights groups are counted under International Organizations.

Other types of organizations commanding at least 5 percent of social justice grant dollars included educational institutions (12.1 percent), which encompasses education policy and reform organizations, and multipurpose human service agencies (11.6 percent), human rights groups (9.4 percent), public affairs and public administration agencies (8.5 percent), housing development and rights organizations (7.2 percent), and health organizations (6.1 percent).

The breakdown of social justice giving by recipient type and number of grants provides a somewhat different picture of funding priorities. Economic and community development organizations still captured the largest share of funding (17.8 percent), but they were followed by housing development and rights organizations (15.2 percent) and human rights groups (14.4 percent). Among leading recipient organizations in these categories were Habitat for Humanity International, with 88 grants totaling $15.2 million; and Human Rights Watch, with 36 grants totaling $8.4 million (Table 4-26). Other organizations receiving more than 5 percent of social justice grants included international organizations (9.6 percent), educational institutions (8.7 percent), human service agencies (7 percent), public affairs/public administration agencies (6.3 percent), and legal services and criminal justice organizations (6.2 percent).

TABLE 4-25 Distribution of Social Justice Giving by Recipient Type, 2006

Recipient Type	Dollar Value of Grants	%	No. of Grants	%
Economic/Community Development Organizations	**$380,443**	**16.5**	**2,730**	**17.8**
International Organizations	**380,197**	**16.5**	**1,462**	**9.6**
Economic Development Organizations	161,745	7.0	394	2.6
Human Rights Organizations	68,540	3.0	379	2.5
Peace and Security Organizations	34,212	1.5	206	1.3
Other	115699	5.0	483	3.2
Educational Institutions	**279,626**	**12.1**	**1,326**	**8.7**
Higher and Graduate Educational Institutions	167,683	7.2	775	5.1
Educational Reform Agencies	88,284	3.8	451	2.9
Other	23,658	1.1	100	0.7
Human Service Agencies—Multipurpose	**266,455**	**11.6**	**1,078**	**7.0**
Human Rights and Civil Liberties Groups[1]	**215,513**	**9.4**	**2,197**	**14.4**
Public Affairs/Administration Agencies	**195,587**	**8.5**	**966**	**6.3**
Housing Development/Rights Organizations	**164,817**	**7.2**	**2,326**	**15.2**
Health Organizations	**141,287**	**6.1**	**714**	**4.7**
Public/General Health Organizations	105,757	4.6	440	2.9
Hospitals/Medical Care Facilities	24,507	1.1	187	1.2
Other	11,022	0.4	87	0.5
Legal Services/Criminal Justice Organizations	**78,726**	**3.4**	**951**	**6.2**
Environment/Environmental Justice Agencies	**32,272**	**1.4**	**290**	**1.9**
Employment Development and Rights Organizations	**23,137**	**1.4**	**275**	**1.8**
Media Organizations	**14,420**	**0.6**	**134**	**0.9**
Social Science Organizations	**38,331**	**1.7**	**177**	**1.2**
Philanthropy Organizations	**37,015**	**1.6**	**167**	**1.1**
Other	**52,929**	**2.2**	**509**	**3.3**
Total	$2,300,762	100.0	15,302	100.0

Source: The Foundation Center, *Social Justice Grantmaking II*, 2009. Based on all grants of $10,000 or more awarded by a sample of 871 larger foundations. Grants may benefit multiple population groups, e.g., a grant for homeless women and their children, and therefore figures are only representative.

[1] Human rights and civil liberties groups includes only domestic organizations; international human rights groups are counted under International Organizations.

International organizations (up 167.3 percent) and human service agencies (up 165.3 percent) led based on growth in social justice grant dollars between 2002 and 2006 (Figure 4-17). Other areas reporting above-average growth included philanthropy-related organizations (up 77.3 percent), public affairs and public administration agencies (up 63.4 percent), and environment and environmental justice organizations (up 50.9 percent).

In contrast, health organizations experienced a slight decline in grant dollars (3.5 percent) but benefited from an above-average increase in the number of grants (18.8 percent). Three other recipient types showing decreased grant dollars in the latest period included educational institutions (down 6.9 percent), social science organizations (down 15.2 percent), and the media (down 36.1 percent).

TABLE 4-26 | Top 50 Recipients of Social Justice Giving, 2006

Recipient	State/Country	Amount	No. of Grants	Recipient	State/Country	Amount	No. of Grants
1. Alliance for a Green Revolution in Africa	Kenya	$150,000,000	6	26. Human Rights Watch	NY	8,437,834	36
2. Bangladesh Rural Advance Commission (BRAC)	Bangladesh	40,167,972	2	27. Nuclear Threat Initiative	DC	8,100,000	3
3. United Nations Foundation	DC	39,997,372	14	28. University of New Mexico Foundation	NM	8,000,000	1
4. International Bank for Reconstruction and Development	DC	28,285,956	3	29. Big Thought	TX	8,000,000	1
5. Carnegie Endowment for International Peace	DC	19,976,848	18	30. Harvard University	MA	7,906,041	34
6. International Rescue Committee	NY	17,233,031	66	31. San Diego Revitalization Corporation	CA	7,744,563	5
7. Habitat for Humanity International	GA	15,179,854	88	32. Children's Defense Fund	DC	7,615,350	21
8. Local Initiatives Support Corporation (LISC)	NY	14,476,793	58	33. National Women's Law Center	DC	7,585,000	29
9. International Development Enterprises	CO	13,687,709	5	34. One Economy Corporation	DC	7,264,650	23
10. Center for Global Development	DC	12,863,638	13	35. Enterprise Community Partners	MD	7,234,500	34
11. Public Interest Projects	NY	12,220,000	22	36. Corporation for Supportive Housing	NY	7,127,500	8
12. Asian Vegetable Research and Development Center	Taiwan	12,083,990	1	37. International Center for Transitional Justice	NY	7,121,500	11
13. Manpower Demonstration Research Corporation (MDRC)	NY	11,793,515	31	38. Focus: Hope	MI	6,791,000	21
14. ActionAid USA	DC	11,106,823	5	39. Enterprise Corporation of the Delta	MS	6,600,000	15
15. Center on Budget and Policy Priorities	DC	10,832,070	32	40. Council of Michigan Foundations	MI	6,500,000	1
16. United Nations High Commissioner for Refugees	Switzerland	10,050,875	2	41. Southern Education Foundation	GA	6,408,800	5
17. California, State of	CA	10,000,000	1	42. MicroSave India	India	6,322,709	1
18. Turtle Mountain Band of Chippewa Indians	ND	10,000,000	1	43. PATH	WA	6,279,480	3
19. New York University	NY	9,845,266	20	44. Guttmacher Institute	NY	6,164,813	24
20. Cheyenne River Sioux Tribe	SD	9,500,000	1	45. Washington DC Martin Luther King, Jr. National Memorial Project Foundation	DC	6,035,000	12
21. National Council of La Raza	DC	9,379,221	43	46. University Research Corporation International	MD	5,997,773	1
22. Living Cities: The National Community Development Initiative	NY	9,332,000	12	47. Global Development Network	DC	5,956,143	1
23. Families USA Foundation	DC	8,987,642	13	48. National Partnership for Women and Families	DC	5,892,398	13
24. University of North Carolina	NC	8,905,892	13	49. Stanford University	CA	5,870,573	18
25. Joint Center for Political and Economic Studies	DC	8,480,150	16	50. International Maize and Wheat Improvement Center	Mexico	5,800,000	1

Source: The Foundation Center, *Social Justice Grantmaking II*, 2009. Based on all grants of $10,000 or more awarded by a sample of 871 larger foundations. Grant reporting period covers fiscal year 2006 for some foundations and 2005 for others.

SOCIAL JUSTICE GRANTMAKING IN THE AFTERMATH OF THE GULF COAST HURRICANES

In the first two years following the devastation wrought by hurricanes Katrina and Rita, institutional donors—including corporations, private and public foundations, and associations—committed over $1 billion in cash and in-kind support to assist in relief, recovery, and rebuilding efforts.[1] This represented exceptional giving for most of these grantmakers, as few foundations identify disaster-response funding as part of their core missions.

Although the majority of the disaster-response giving has provided for basic human service needs, along with education and health, the clear racial and economic disparities highlighted by the disaster have led some funders to address the recovery and rebuilding efforts from a social justice perspective. In fact, the private and community foundations included in the 2006 Foundation Center grants sample alone awarded 135 grants totaling $33 million for social justice-related efforts in the aftermath of the 2005 Gulf Coast hurricanes.

The Ford Foundation awarded the largest amount of social justice funding in response to the disaster ($5.8 million). Among Ford's 25 grants was a $200,000 award to Tulane University's Institute for the Study of Race and Poverty in New Orleans to promote social change through the reduction of racially based economic disparities, and to contribute to the rejuvenation of New Orleans. The W.K. Kellogg Foundation ranked second and provided eight social justice-related grants as part of its efforts to support the Gulf Coast recovery, including a $200,000 award to the PICO Network to enable working families and low- and moderate-income communities to have a voice in the rebuilding of Louisiana.

Finally, while social justice-related grantmaking in the aftermath of hurricanes Katrina and Rita seeks to ensure an equitable future for the historically disadvantaged populations of the Gulf Coast region, at least one funder has sought to achieve that goal by better understanding why the disaster unfolded as it did. Through a $25,000 grant to New Orleans-based Dillard University, the Fannie Mae Foundation supported a symposium entitled "Race, Place, and the Environment After Katrina: Looking Back to Look Forward" to explore the racial disparities in disaster preparedness, response, cleanup, debris management, recovery, rebuilding, reconstruction, and the repopulation of New Orleans.

Endnote

1. See Lawrence, S., et al., *Giving in the Aftermath of the Gulf Coast Hurricanes: Update on the Foundation and Corporate Response*, New York: Foundation Center, 2007.

Social Justice Giving by Region

- Northeastern and Western foundations accounted for the biggest shares of dollars awarded in 2006

- Foundations in the West provided a larger share of grant dollars awarded

Foundations based in the Northeast continued to provide the largest share of social justice giving in 2006— 35.6 percent—but this share was down from more than 44 percent in 2002 (Figure 4-18). By comparison, foundations in the West boosted their share of social justice funding during this period from less than 20 percent to over 31 percent. Following these regions were the Midwest (21.2 percent) and the South (9.9 percent).[11]

Increased social justice-related giving by the Washington State-based Bill & Melinda Gates Foundation explained most of the larger share of support provided by Western foundations in 2006. However, several other funders in the region also posted substantial increases in giving; among them were the Evelyn and Walter Haas, Jr. Fund and Peninsula Community Foundation.[12]

Consistent with findings based on the source of funding, recipient organizations located in the Northeast and West regions benefited from the largest shares of social justice grant dollars in 2006 (24.9 percent and 22.8 percent, respectively). Smaller shares were received by organizations in the South (14.5 percent) and the Midwest (12.2 percent). Yet despite minor fluctuations, these shares remained remarkably consistent with 2002 shares.

In addition to the four major regions cited above, organizations based in Washington, DC commanded 25.7 percent of the overall social justice dollars ($475 million), reflecting the concentration of national and international organizations involved in social justice issues in that city. California ($320.8 million) and New York ($305.7 million) also benefited from large shares of social justice support, reflecting a similar concentration of major social justice organizations in San Francisco, Los Angeles, and New York City.

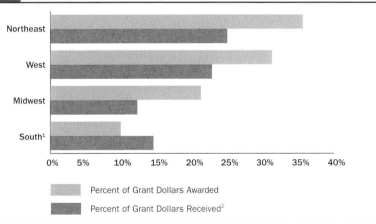

FIGURE 4-18 Distribution of Social Justice Giving by Region, 2006

Percent of Grant Dollars Awarded
Percent of Grant Dollars Received[2]

Source: The Foundation Center, Social Justice Grantmaking II, 2009. Based on all grants of $10,000 or more awarded by a sample of 871 larger foundations. Excludes giving by operating foundations.
[1]Figures for the South exclude the District of Columbia. DC-based foundations provided 2.4 percent of grant dollars in the sample and DC-based organizations received 14.7 percent of grant dollars in the sample.
[2]A total of 11.7 percent of grant dollars was provided to overseas recipients.

Social Justice Giving by Types of Support

The Foundation Center's grants classification system tracks the purpose of grants across eight major type-of-support categories: general support, capital support, program support, research, student aid funds[13] (excluding grants paid directly to individuals), technical assistance, emergency funds, and program evaluation. The system also tracks two qualifying types of support—continuing support and matching or challenge grants.[14] Because grants may be tracked under more than one type of support (e.g., a grant for operating support and capital equipment), each category is analyzed as a percentage of the total grant dollars and number of grants represented in the social justice sample.

- Nearly three-quarters of social justice giving supported specific programs and projects in 2006

- Program and general support showed above-average growth between 2002 and 2006

In 2006, close to three-quarters (73.6 percent) of social justice grant dollars and three-fifths (60.1 percent) of grants provided funding for specific programs and projects (Figure 4-19 and Table 4-27). These shares significantly exceeded the

TABLE 4-27 | Social Justice Giving by Types of Support, 2006

Type of Support	Amount	%	No. of Grants	%
General Support	**$468,038**	**20.3**	**3,377**	**22.1**
General/Operating Support	370,831	16.1	2,847	18.6
Management Development	66,921	2.9	381	2.5
Income Development	30,107	1.3	143	0.9
Annual Campaigns	178	0.0	6	0.0
Capital Support	**129,087**	**5.6**	**648**	**4.2**
Building/Renovations	54,878	2.4	365	2.4
Endowments	33,708	1.5	21	0.1
Capital Campaigns	14,849	0.6	63	0.4
Computer Systems/Equipment	11,062	0.5	112	0.7
Land Acquisition	9,570	0.4	20	0.1
Equipment	4,390	0.2	65	0.4
Debt Reduction	428	0.0	1	0.0
Collections Acquisition	200	0.0	1	0.0
Program Support	**1,693,911**	**73.6**	**9,197**	**60.1**
Program Development	1,506,176	65.5	7,742	50.6
Electronic Median/Online Services	47,871	2.1	193	1.3
Faculty/Staff Development	35,470	1.5	226	1.5
Conferences/Seminars	35,098	1.5	424	2.8
Publication	27,054	1.2	253	1.7
Seed Money	13,901	0.6	114	0.7
Curriculum Development	14,740	0.6	70	0.5
Film/Video/Radio	9,506	0.4	120	0.8
Exhibitions	1,947	0.1	29	0.2
Collections Management/Preservation	1,471	0.1	8	0.1
Performance/Productions	393	0.0	13	0.1
Commissioning New Works	215	0.0	3	0.0
Professorships	65	0.0	2	0.0
Research	**297,400**	**12.9**	**1,211**	**7.9**
Student Aid Funds	**41,295**	**1.8**	**219**	**1.4**
Fellowships	20,506	0.9	79	0.5
Internship Funds	10,914	0.5	22	0.1
Awards/Prizes/Competitions	6,134	0.3	76	0.5
Student Aid	2,017	0.1	13	0.1
Scholarship Funds	1,722	0.1	29	0.2
Technical Assistance	**51,100**	**2.2**	**200**	**1.3**
Other	**40,038**	**1.7**	**121**	**0.8**
Program Evaluation	39,998	1.7	119	0.8
Emergency Funds	40	0.0	2	0.0
Not Specified	**152,843**	**6.6**	**2,629**	**17.2**
Qualifying Support Type[1]				
Continuing	430,447	18.7	3,517	23.0
Matching or Challenge	18,381	0.8	76	0.5

Source: The Foundation Center, *Social Justice Grantmaking II*, 2009. Based on all grants of $10,000 or more awarded by a sample of 871 larger foundations. Grants may occasionally be for multiple types of support and would therefore be counted more than once.
[1]Qualifying types of support are tracked in addition to basic types of support, e.g., a challenge grant for construction, and are therefore represented separately.

50 percent of grant dollars and roughly two-fifths of grants coded for program support in the overall sample. Among other types of support, funders in the sample also allocated larger shares of their social justice grant dollars for general operating support (20.3 percent versus 19.0 percent) and research (12.9 percent versus 8.8 percent), while providing a much smaller share for capital support (5.6 percent versus 17.7 percent).

Between 2002 and 2006, above-average growth in social justice grant dollars and grants was reported for both program and general support (Figure 4-20). Program support dollars rose 117.9 percent and the number of grants by 60.2 percent, while general support dollars increased 40.7 percent and the number of grants by 43.2 percent. In contrast, social justice-related support for research declined 15.6 percent, and technical assistance dollars declined 9.4 percent.

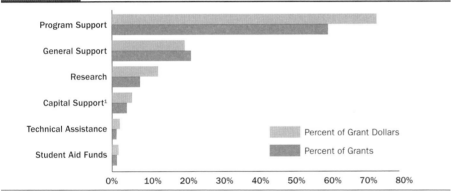

FIGURE 4-19 Social Justice Giving by Major Types of Support, 2006

Source: The Foundation Center, *Social Justice Grantmaking II*, 2009. Based on all grants of $10,000 or more awarded by a sample of 871 larger foundations.
¹Includes endowment funds.

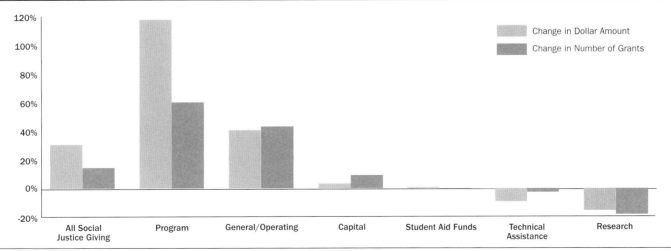

FIGURE 4-20 Change in Social Justice Giving by Major Types of Support, 2002 and 2006

Source: The Foundation Center, *Social Justice Grantmaking II*, 2009. Based on all grants of $10,000 or more awarded by a sample of 749 larger foundations for 2002 and 871 for 2006.

PUBLIC FOUNDATION SOCIAL JUSTICE FUNDERS

◆ **30 leading funders provided close to $116 million in 2006**

◆ **Tides Foundation dominated funding**

Private and community foundations account for the vast majority of institutional philanthropic support for social justice-related activities but are far from the only source of funding. Numerous grantmaking public charities, also known as public foundations, have been established for the purpose of making grants to advance social justice broadly or for the benefit of specific populations. Unlike private foundations, however, these organizations raise their grant dollars from a variety of donors, including private foundations, and their close-to-the-ground knowledge is attractive to other donors. In fact, private and community foundations included in the Foundation Center's 2006 grants sample provided 285 grants totaling $43.1 million to the public foundations listed in Table 4-X1.[1]

To illuminate the role of public foundations in supporting social justice, the Foundation Center has prepared a brief examination of the grantmaking priorities of a set of these funds. Overall, 30 of the leading public foundation social justice funders made more than 6,600 grants totaling $115.6 million in 2006. To be included in this set, the missions of these organizations had to indicate a primary focus on social justice-related goals, and their activities had to principally—although not exclusively—focus on grantmaking.[2]

Surprisingly, less than 45 percent of their 2006 grant dollars and grants met the definition of social justice philanthropy

used to identify grantmaking by private foundations. A closer examination of grants that did not meet the social justice definition suggests that more detailed descriptions of these awards by the funders would have led to most of them being captured by the definition. For this reason, all of the giving by these institutions has been included in this analysis.

The San Francisco-based Tides Foundation accounted for well over half of grant dollars and close to one-third of the number of grants awarded by the set of 30 selected funds in 2006. The foundation, which seeks "to promote economic justice, robust democratic processes, and the opportunity to live in a healthy and sustainable environment where human rights are preserved and protected," receives support for its activities from individual donors and private foundations, as well as other public foundations.[3] A number of funds were created to benefit specific population groups, such as women (e.g., Global Fund for Women, Ms. Foundation for Women), People of Color (e.g., Twenty-First Century Foundation), and LGBT populations (e.g., Pride Foundation, Stonewall Community Foundation). However, while these 30 funds represent most of the largest public foundation social justice funders based on grant dollars, they represent only a fraction of the number of funds serving similar missions.

Human rights and civil liberties captured by far the largest share of giving awarded by the selected public foundation social justice funders in 2006 (Figure 4-X1). Economic development, human services, and the environment followed with roughly one-tenth shares of grant dollars. However, when the largest funder in the set—the Tides Foundation—was excluded, different grantmaking patterns emerged. For

TABLE 4-X1 Selected Public Foundation Social Justice Funders, 2006*

Foundation	State	Amount	%	No. of Grants	%	Foundation	State	Amount	%	No. of Grants	%
1. Tides Foundation[1]	CA	$65,284,520	56.5	2,169	32.7	**17.** North Star Fund	NY	1,030,560	0.9	75	1.1
2. Global Fund for Women	CA	7,724,504	6.7	640	9.7	**18.** Southern Partners Fund	GA	1,002,994	0.9	94	1.4
3. Proteus Fund	MA	5,487,691	4.7	167	2.5	**19.** Stonewall Community Foundation	NY	915,053	0.8	83	1.3
4. New World Foundation	NY	4,393,996	3.8	177	2.7	**20.** Threshold Foundation	CA	824,514	0.7	34	0.5
5. Ms. Foundation for Women	NY	3,813,039	3.3	151	2.3	**21.** Pride Foundation	WA	811,706	0.7	356	5.4
6. Funding Exchange	NY	3,283,308	2.8	472	7.1	**22.** First Nations Development Institute	CO	680,576	0.6	38	0.6
7. Liberty Hill Foundation	CA	2,947,470	2.5	454	6.8	**23.** Jewish Funds for Justice	NY	620,000	0.5	40	0.6
8. ZeroDivide	CA	2,420,803	2.1	112	1.7	**24.** Social Justice Fund Northwest	WA	578,327	0.5	89	1.3
9. Horizons Foundation	CA	1,717,581	1.5	306	4.6	**25.** Community Shares of Wisconsin	WI	525,904	0.5	57	0.9
10. Astraea Lesbian Foundation for Justice	NY	1,705,201	1.5	168	2.5	**26.** Haymarket People's Fund	MA	478,649	0.4	109	1.6
11. Vanguard Public Foundation	CA	1,588,603	1.4	190	2.9	**27.** Headwaters Foundation for Justice	MN	470,000	0.4	61	0.9
12. Twenty-First Century Foundation	NY	1,441,056	1.2	100	1.5	**28.** Community Shares Minnesota	MN	417,708	0.4	40	0.6
13. Women's Foundation of California	CA	1,380,500	1.2	90	1.4	**29.** Crossroads Fund	IL	361,526	0.3	45	0.7
14. Agape Foundation	CA	1,206,953	1.0	78	1.2	**30.** McKenzie River Gathering Foundation	OR	350,000	0.3	55	0.8
15. Grassroots International	MA	1,139,986	1.0	75	1.1						
16. Women's Foundation of Minnesota	MN	1,033,117	0.9	104	1.6	**Total**		**$115,635,845**	**100.0**	**6,629**	**100.0**

Source: The Foundation Center, *Social Justice Grantmaking II*, 2009. Figures based on all grants awarded by selected funders.
*Grants awarded by any of the 30 public foundations included in the set to other public foundations in the set have been excluded to avoid double-counting grants.
[1]Figures include grants made through the Tides Center.

example, while human rights and civil liberties continued to account for the largest share of grant dollars among the 29 other funds, its share of giving rose to almost 30 percent; and human services moved into the second-rank position with close to 17 percent of grant dollars.

Finally, the majority (71.4 percent) of 2006 giving by the selected public foundation social justice funders targeted domestic activities. Nonetheless, five out of six funders made at least one international grant, with one-third reporting more than 10 international grants. The top five funders by number of international grants included the Tides Foundation, Global Fund for Women, Astraea Lesbian Foundation for Justice, Funding Exchange, and Grassroots International. By grant dollars, the Tides Foundation ranked first, followed by the Global Fund for Women and Grassroots International.

Endnotes

1. Of the $43.1 million awarded, $24.5 million (56.8 percent) met the definition for social justice-related giving used in this report. Private foundations also provide social justice-related support to organizations that do not primarily serve as grantmakers for the purpose of regranting, such as grantmaker networks (e.g., Asian Americans/Pacific Islanders in Philanthropy, Funders for Lesbian and Gay Issues, and the Women's Funding Network).
2. The 30 public foundation social justice funders included in this analysis were identified based on their being U.S.-based organizations that primarily serve as grantmakers, maintaining an explicit focus on social justice-related activities, and ranking among top funders of this type based on grant dollars awarded overall or based on support provided to them by private foundations. Additional funders were included based on recommendations by project advisors. While this set includes most of the leading public foundation social justice funders, it is not intended to be comprehensive. Therefore, findings should be interpreted as being suggestive of grantmaking trends by these types of public foundations but not representative.
3. For the purpose of this analysis, grants awarded by any of the 30 public foundations included in the set to other public foundations in the set have been excluded to avoid double-counting grants.

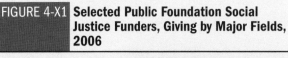

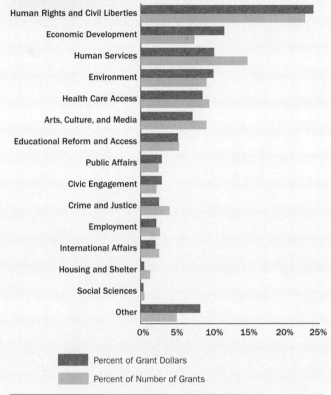

FIGURE 4-X1 Selected Public Foundation Social Justice Funders, Giving by Major Fields, 2006

Human Rights and Civil Liberties
Economic Development
Human Services
Environment
Health Care Access
Arts, Culture, and Media
Educational Reform and Access
Public Affairs
Civic Engagement
Crime and Justice
Employment
International Affairs
Housing and Shelter
Social Sciences
Other

0% 5% 10% 15% 20% 25%

■ Percent of Grant Dollars
■ Percent of Number of Grants

Source: The Foundation Center, *Social Justice Grantmaking II*, 2009. Figures based on all grants awarded by 30 selected funders.
[1]Includes support for U.S.-based international programs and recipients in other countries.

ENDNOTES

1. Giving by the sampled foundations represented roughly half of the $39 billion awarded by the universe of over 72,000 grantmaking foundations in 2006.
2. The Peninsula Community Foundation merged with Community Foundation Silicon Valley in 2007 to form the Silicon Valley Community Foundation.
3. Formerly named Programs for a Green Revolution in Africa.
4. The foundation was not included in the 2002 social justice sample.
5. The analysis of funding for social justice by field uses a modified version of the National Taxonomy of Exempt Entities (NTEE), adapted by the Foundation Center for its grants classification system. Social justice grantmaking is divided in 14 major fields, reflecting the principal areas of social justice giving. Support for international activities and policy-related funding are captured within all of the major fields. See Appendix B for a complete description of the social justice taxonomy. The specialized taxonomy was developed by the Foundation Center in conjunction

with INDEPENDENT SECTOR and the project's 2005 advisory committee for the first edition of *Social Justice Grantmaking*.

6. Support includes only grants targeted to improving educational opportunities for a class of individuals—e.g., economically disadvantaged students. It does not include funding for scholarship programs that target individuals.
7. The Peninsula Community Foundation merged with Community Foundation Silicon Valley in 2007 to form the Silicon Valley Community Foundation.
8. The foundation ceased operation in January 2009.
9. Among grants not coded for specific population groups are those that provide for the general support of institutions or programs that serve broad public interests (e.g., community centers), although multiple target groups may derive a benefit; and for the category of children and youth, grants for the general support of elementary and secondary schools, college scholarships, and general recreational agencies, such as YMCAs and YWCAs, since these grants serve a broader community than children and youth.
10. Grant dollars targeted to units or departments of larger institutions, e.g., to a university library or to a graduate program within a university, are

counted as dollars to the primary organization, in this case, a university.

11. Figures for the South exclude the District of Columbia. DC-based foundations provided 2 percent of social justice grant dollars, while DC-based organizations received 25.7 percent of grant dollars in 2006.
12. The Peninsula Community Foundation merged with Community Foundation Silicon Valley in 2007 to form the Silicon Valley Community Foundation.
13. Based on the recommendation of advisors to the 2005 *Social Justice Grantmaking* study, grants for student aid funds that benefit disadvantaged populations were not automatically included in the social justice set. See Educational Reform and Access for details on educational grants included in the set.
14. In most cases, grants assigned a qualifying type of support code are double-coded, e.g., a grant for a capital campaign that is awarded on a challenge basis.

Appendix A
Study Methodology

Information for *Social Justice Grantmaking II* was gathered principally from the Foundation Center's grants database and a survey of grantmakers conducted in 2008.

IDENTIFYING SOCIAL JUSTICE GRANTS

As detailed in Chapter 1, the Center worked closely with INDEPENDENT SECTOR and the original project advisors to map their working definition of social justice philanthropy to the Center's grants sample data. Much of this work entailed reviewing thousands of individual grant records to determine the suitability of "objective" codes to capturing the intent of the social justice philanthropy definition.

The mapping takes advantage of the National Taxonomy of Exempt Entities (NTEE), a coding system developed to classify nonprofit organizations and activities. (See Appendix B for a detailed description of the Grants Classification System.) Beyond NTEE's basic field coding, the mapping of INDEPENDENT SECTOR's social justice definition also utilized the Center's practice of separately coding the primary and secondary purpose of grants, the primary and secondary purpose of recipient organizations, the special population groups intended to benefit from grants (when known), and the geographic focus of grants. Using these tools, INDEPENDENT SECTOR, the Center, and the project's advisors agreed on an "objective" definition of social justice-related grantmaking that encompassed all:

- domestic or international grants with a primary or secondary grant purpose or recipient type code for civil rights, human rights, civil liberties, equal opportunity and access (in all subject areas), poverty research, and election regulation.

- domestic or international grants with a primary or secondary grant purpose or recipient type code for educational reform, health care financing, labor organizing, housing development and owner/renter support, urban/rural community and economic development, community improvement coalitions, technical assistance for community development, public affairs research, government reform and financing, leadership development, public policy (in all subject areas), and reform (in all subject areas) that specify a benefit for "core population groups" (these include the aging/elderly/senior citizens, disabled, economically disadvantaged, ethnic and racial minorities, gays and lesbians, immigrants and refugees, and women and girls).

- domestic or international grants with a primary grant purpose of general community development that specify a benefit for "core population groups" (see above).

- domestic or international grants with a primary grant purpose or recipient type code for general economic development that specify a benefit for "core population groups" (see above).

- domestic or international grants with a primary or secondary grant purpose or recipient type code for court reform, legal services, and public interest law that specify a benefit for offenders/ex-offenders or the "core population groups" (see above).

- domestic grants with a primary purpose of civic participation.

- international grants with a primary or secondary grant purpose or recipient type code for human rights, peace and security, educational reform, health care financing, court reform, legal services, public interest law, labor organizing, and leadership development.

- international grants with a primary or secondary purpose of civil society/civic participation.

- international grants with a primary purpose of general community development, economic development, and agricultural development.

The definition developed for this analysis provides the most comprehensive accounting available of foundations' social justice-related grantmaking. Still, this definition may exclude giving that some funders would consider social justice-related, while capturing the grants of foundations that do not necessarily think of themselves as social justice funders. In addition, limitations in the information provided by some foundations (e.g., grant records lacking text descriptions) mean that not all social justice-related giving based on the "objective" definition developed for this project may be captured in the analysis.

THE FOUNDATION CENTER'S GRANTS SAMPLE

Chapter 4 of this report analyzes trends in social justice grantmaking between 2002 and 2006. This analysis was based on the Foundation Center's grants database, which includes all of the grants of $10,000 or more awarded by a sample of mostly large and mid-size foundations.

In the 2006 reporting year, the grants database included 1,263 foundations and more than 140,000 grants. Giving by these funders totaled $19.1 billion, or about one-half of all U.S. foundation giving. The sample included grants awarded or paid in 2006 for a majority of grantmakers. (The remaining funders were represented by 2005 data.)

For the 2002 reporting year, the grants database included 1,005 foundations and nearly 128,000 grants. Foundations in this sample provided grants totaling $15.9 billion, or a similar roughly one-half share of all foundation giving in that year. The majority of funders were represented with 2002 grants, with the balance reflecting 2001 grants data. (For more detailed information on the grants sample, see *Foundation Giving Trends: Update on Funding Priorities*.)

Limitations of the Grants Sample

The Foundation Center's grants database is the most complete source of information available about foundation giving, capturing about half of all grant dollars awarded by U.S. foundations. Still, it has certain limitations:

1. The sample is not randomly selected; rather it covers the grants of roughly 800 of the 1,000 largest foundations, the top 15 funders in each state plus an additional set of smaller foundations reporting voluntarily to the Foundation Center. As a result, the sample is weighted toward large foundations.

2. The sample includes a high proportion of corporate foundations, which represent about one in six of the over 1,000 largest foundations in the sample; and of community foundations, which account for many of the smallest funders in the sample.

3. The grants database includes only unrestricted and donor-advised grants from community foundations. It excludes grants from donor-designated and restricted funds. Therefore, social justice-related giving by some community foundations may be underrepresented.

4. The sample excludes grants under $10,000. Therefore, funding amounts of foundations that award a high proportion of small grants are underreported. Similarly, funding trends associated with small grants may be underreported.

5. The grants database includes grants authorized (when known) rather than grants paid. Because the study compares changes in grants awarded over a four-year interval, large multi-year grants authorized in intervening years do not appear in the trends data.

6. The sample includes only grants awarded to organizations. Grants or fellowships given directly to individuals are excluded.

7. The Center has not attempted to consistently include all of the largest foundations. For example, in some years individual foundations are omitted from the file for lack of timely information or if their grants information is incomplete.

A Framework for Presenting Social Justice Grantmaking

To facilitate the analysis of programmatic funding patterns, a subject framework was devised for social justice-related grantmaking. The framework was created using NTEE grant subject codes. See Appendix B for a complete description of the NTEE system and listing of the social justice taxonomy.

SURVEY OF SOCIAL JUSTICE GRANTMAKERS

To complement the descriptive, quantitative components of the study, the project commissioned a survey of leading social justice grantmakers and practitioners. The purpose of the survey was to gain a more nuanced understanding of funders' perspectives on recent issues and developments in social justice grantmaking. Eighteen funders and eight practitioners participated in interviews conducted during the summer and fall of 2008. Participating institutions are listed on page iv. The analysis is presented in Chapter 2.

While the sample is too small to formulate any definitive conclusions, the results of the survey are nonetheless useful in gaining insights into funder perspectives on the issues in the field, as well as evolving changes in the practices of selected social justice philanthropy leaders.

Appendix B
The Grants Classification System: Tracking Social Justice Grants

Since the 1970s, the Foundation Center has collected and published summary information on international grants as part of its grants indexing system.

The current system is based on the National Taxonomy of Exempt Entities (NTEE) classification system, a coding scheme developed by the National Center for Charitable Statistics that uses two- or three-character alphanumeric codes to track institutional fields and entities, governance or auspices, population groups, and religious affiliations. The universe of institutional fields is organized into 26 "major field" areas (A to Z), defined below. The first letter of each code denotes the field, such as "A" for Arts, "B" for Education, and "R" for Civil Rights/Social Action.

A Modified Taxonomy for Social Justice Grants

This report uses a modified version of the standard NTEE classification system to provide a more detailed analysis of social justice grantmaking by subject. The new subject taxonomy organizes social justice-related grants into 15 major topics and 29 subtopics. This revised structure allows for presenting topics that dominate social justice grantmaking—e.g., Economic and Community Development, Health Care Access and Affordability, and Civil Rights and Civil Liberties—in greater detail than the standard NTEE format. These modifications ensure that the analysis is more inclusive and comprehensible to those active in the social justice field.

Standard NTEE Classification by Subject

A—Arts, culture, humanities activities
- arts & culture (multipurpose activities)
- media & communications
- visual arts
- museums
- performing arts
- humanities
- historical societies & related historical activities

B—Educational institutions & related activities
- elementary & secondary education (preschool through Grade 12)
- vocational/technical schools
- higher education
- graduate/professional schools
- adult/continuing education
- libraries/archives
- student services & organizations

C—Environmental quality, protection
- pollution abatement & control
- natural resources conservation & protection
- botanic/horticulture activities
- environmental beautification & open spaces
- environmental education & outdoor survival

D—Animal-related activities
- animal protection & welfare
- humane societies
- wildlife preservation & protection
- veterinary services
- zoos & aquariums
- specialty animals & other services

E—Health—general & rehabilitative
- hospitals
- health treatment, primarily outpatient
- reproductive health care
- rehabilitative medical services
- health support services
- emergency medical services
- public health & wellness education
- health care financing/insurance programs
- nursing homes/nursing care

F—Mental health, crisis intervention
- addiction prevention & treatment
- mental health treatment & services
- crisis intervention
- psychiatric/mental health—primary care
- half-way houses (mental health)/transitional care
- counseling/bereavement services
- specific mental health disorders

G—Disease/disorder/medical disciplines (multipurpose)
- birth defects & genetic diseases
- cancer
- diseases of specific organs
- nerve, muscle & bone diseases
- allergy-related diseases
- specific named diseases
- medical disciplines/specialties

H—Medical research
- identical hierarchy to diseases/disorders/medical disciplines in major field "G"
- example: G30 represents American Cancer Society; H30 represents cancer research

I—Public protection: crime/courts/legal services
- police & law enforcement agencies
- correctional facilities & prisoner services
- crime prevention
- rehabilitation of offenders
- administration of justice/courts
- protection against/prevention of neglect, abuse, exploitation
- legal services

J—Employment/jobs
- vocational guidance & training, such as on-the-job programs
- employment procurement assistance
- vocational rehabilitation
- employment assistance for the disabled and aging
- labor unions/organizations
- labor-management relations

K—Food, nutrition, agriculture
- agricultural services aimed at food procurement
- food service/free food distribution
- nutrition promotion
- farmland preservation

L—Housing/shelter
- housing development/construction
- housing search assistance
- low-cost temporary shelters such as youth hostels
- homeless, temporary shelter for
- housing owners/renters organizations
- housing support services

M—Public safety/disaster preparedness & relief
- disaster prevention, such as flood control
- disaster relief (U.S. domestic)
- safety education
- civil defense & preparedness programs

N—Recreation, leisure, sports, athletics
- camps
- physical fitness & community recreation
- sports training
- recreation/pleasure or social clubs
- amateur sports
- Olympics & Special Olympics
- professional athletic leagues

O—Youth development
- youth centers, such as boys clubs
- scouting
- mentoring (including Big Brothers/Sisters)
- agricultural development, such as 4-H
- business development, Junior Achievement
- citizenship programs
- religious leadership development

P—Human service—other/multipurpose
- multipurpose service organizations
- children & youth services
- family services
- personal social services
- emergency assistance (food, clothing)
- residential/custodial care (including hospices)
- centers promoting independence of specific groups, such as senior or women's centers

Q—International
- exchange programs
- international development
- international relief services (foreign disaster relief)
- peace & security (international conflict resolution)
- foreign policy research & analyses
- international human rights

R—Civil rights/civil liberties
- equal opportunity & access
- intergroup/race relations
- voter education/registration
- civil liberties

S—Community improvement/development
- community/neighborhood development
- community coalitions
- economic development, both urban and rural
- business services
- nonprofit management
- community service clubs such as Junior League

T—Philanthropy & voluntarism
- philanthropy associations/societies
- private grantmaking foundations
- public foundations (e.g., women's funds) and community foundations
- voluntarism promotion
- community funds and federated giving

U—Science
- scientific research & promotion
- physical/earth sciences
- engineering/technology
- biological sciences

V—Social sciences
- social science research/studies
- interdisciplinary studies, such as black studies, women's studies, urban studies, etc.

W—Public affairs/society benefit
- public policy research, general
- government & public administration
- transportation systems
- leadership development
- public utilities
- telecommunications (including WWW)
- consumer rights/education
- military/veterans organizations
- financial institutions, services

X—Religion/spiritual development
- Christian churches, missionary societies and related religious bodies
- Jewish synagogues
- other specific religions

Y—Mutual membership benefit organizations
- insurance providers & services (other than health)
- pension/retirement funds
- fraternal beneficiary societies
- cemeteries & burial services

Z99—Unknown, unclassifiable

Modified NTEE Classification
of Social Justice Grants by Subject*

Field	Code
Economic and Community Development	S,Q3_
Economic Development	S30-33, S4_, Q3_
Community/Neighborhood Development	S20-22, S24-25
Management and Technical Aid	S02
Other	S01, S03-19, S5_, S8_, S99
Health Care Access and Affordability	E, F, G, H
Health Care Access and Quality	E01-19, E2_, E3_, E5_, E6_, E85-88, E9_, G_, H_
Health Care Cost and Financing	E80-84
Reproductive Health Care Access	E4_
Mental Health Care Access	F_
Public Health	E7_
Human Rights and Civil Liberties	R, Q7_
Human Rights	R2_, Q7_
Civil Liberties	R60, R62-69
Reproductive Rights	R61
Race/Intergroup Relations	R3_
Other	R01-19, R4_, R99
Education Reform and Access	B
Elementary and Secondary	B2_, B90-95
Higher and Graduate	B4_, B5_
Other	B01-19, B3_, B6_, B7_, B8_, B99
Housing and Shelter	L
Housing Development	L12, L2_
Other	L01-11, L13-19, L3_, L4_, L5_, L8_, L99
Human Services	K, M, N, O, P
Food, Nutrition, Agriculture	K_
Public Safety/Disaster Preparedness & Relief	M_
Recreation, Leisure, Sports, Athletics	N_
Youth Development	O_
Other/Multipurpose	P_

Field	Code
International Affairs, Peace, and Conflict Resolution	Q (excluding Q3_ and Q7_)
Crime and Justice	I
Legal Services	I8_
Administration of Justice/ Courts	I5_, I6_
Other	I01-19, I2_, I3_, I4_, I7_, I99
Social Science Research	V
Civic Engagement	W23-26, W7
Citizen Participation	W24
Election Regulation and Financing	W23, W25-26
Leadership Development	W7_
Public Affairs	W (excluding W23-26, W7_)
Welfare Policy and Reform	W21
Policy and Reform– Multipurpose	W06-07
Government Financing and Administration	W20, W22
Other	W01-05, W08-19, W3_, W4_, W5_, W6_, W8_, W9_
Employment Development and Rights	J
Environment and Environmental Justice	C, D
Arts, Culture, and Media	A
Other	Z

SOURCE: The Foundation Center, *Social Justice Grantmaking II*, 2009.
*The complete NTEE classification system can be found at foundationcenter.org/gainknowledge/grantsclass.

Appendix C
Types of Support Classification

Annual Campaigns—any organized effort by a nonprofit to secure gifts on an annual basis; also called annual appeals.

Awards/Prizes/Competitions*—grants for artists' awards, prizes, competitions, housing, living space, and work space.

Building/Renovation—grants for constructing, renovating, remodeling, or rehabilitating property.

Capital Campaigns—a campaign, usually extending over a period of years, to raise substantial funds for enduring purposes, such as building or endowment funds.

Collections Acquisition—grants to libraries or museums to acquire permanent materials as part of a collection, usually books or art.

Collections Management/ Preservation*—grants for maintenance, preservation, and conservation of materials.

Commissioning New Works*—support for the creation of new artistic works.

Computer Systems/Equipment—grants to purchase or develop automated systems.

Conferences/Seminars—grants to cover the expenses of holding a conference.

Curriculum Development—grants to schools, colleges, universities, and educational support organizations to develop general or discipline-specific curricula.

Debt Reduction—grants to reduce a recipient organization's indebtedness; also referred to as deficit financing. Frequently refers to mortgage payments.

Electronic Media/Online Services**—grants for support of projects on the Internet and World Wide Web, including online publications and databases, development of web sites, electronic networking and messaging services, CD-ROM products, and interactive educational programs.

Emergency Funds—one-time grants to cover immediate short-term funding needs on an emergency basis.

Endowments—bequests or gifts intended to be kept permanently and invested to provide income for continued support of an organization.

Equipment—grants to purchase equipment, furnishings, or other materials.

Exhibitions—grants to museums, libraries, or historical societies specifically to mount an exhibit or to support the installation of a touring exhibit.

Faculty/Staff Development—includes staff training programs.

Fellowships—funds awarded to educational institutions to support fellowship programs.

Film/Video/Radio—grants to fund a film, video, or radio production by a nonprofit resulting from research or projects of interest to the funder.

General Support—funds for general purpose or work of an organization, and funds to cover the day-to-day personnel, administration, and other expenses for an existing program or project.

Income Development*—grants for fundraising, marketing, and to expand audience base.

Internships—usually indicates funds awarded to an institution or organization to support an internship program rather than a grant to an individual.

Land Acquisition—grants to purchase real estate property.

Management*—grants for salaries, staff support and training, strategic and long-range planning, budgeting, and accounting.

Matching or Challenge Grants—grants to match funds provided by another donor, grants paid only if the donee is able to raise additional funds from other sources.

Performance/Productions—grants to cover costs specifically associated with mounting a performing arts production.

Professorships—grants to an educational institution to endow a professorship or chair.

Program Development—grants to support specific projects or programs as opposed to general purpose grants.

Program Evaluation*—grants to evaluate specific projects or programs; both to agencies and to research institutes and other program evaluators.

Publication—grants to fund reports or other publications issued by a nonprofit resulting from research or projects of interest to the funder.

Research—funds awarded to institutions to cover costs of investigations and clinical trials. Research grants for individuals are usually referred to as fellowships.

Scholarships—grants to an educational institution or organization to support a scholarship program, mainly for students at the undergraduate level.

Seed Money—grants to start, establish, or initiate a new project or organization. Seed grants may cover salaries and other operating expenses of a new project. Also known as "start-up funds."

Student Aid—assistance in the form of educational grants, loans, or scholarships.

Technical Aid—operational or management assistance given to nonprofit organizations, including fundraising assistance, budgeting and financial planning, program planning, legal advice, marketing, and other aids to management.

*Categories of support added to this coding system in 1995.
**Category of support added to this coding system in 1999.

Appendix D
Foundation Center Cooperating Collections

FREE FUNDING INFORMATION CENTERS

For free fundraising information and other funding-related technical assistance, visit our Cooperating Collections. Located across the U.S. and in several locations around the world, in libraries, nonprofit resource centers, or other agencies, Cooperating Collections provide visitors with free access to core Foundation Center electronic and print resources and fundraising research guidance, along with access to the Internet and our searchable databases. Many offer workshops and programs for local nonprofits. For the most current contact information, visit foundationcenter.org/collections or call (800) 424-9836. Individual Collection hours vary, so please confirm specifics before paying a visit. No appointment is necessary, and no fee is charged for use of Foundation Center resources.

ALABAMA

Birmingham: Birmingham Public Library, Government Documents Dept., 2100 Park Place (205) 226-3620

Gadsden: Gadsden Public Library, 254 College St. (256) 549-4699

Hoover: Hoover Public Library, 200 Municipal Dr. (205) 444-7800

Huntsville: Huntsville–Madison County Public Library, Information and Periodicals Dept., 915 Monroe St. (256) 532-5940

Mobile: Mobile Public Library, 5555 Grelot Rd. (251) 340-8555

Montgomery: Auburn University at Montgomery, 74-40 East Dr. (334) 244-3200

ALASKA

Anchorage: University of Alaska–Anchorage, Consortium Library, 3211 Providence Dr. (907) 786-1848

Juneau: Juneau Public Library, 292 Marine Way (907) 586-5267

ARIZONA

Flagstaff: Flagstaff City–Coconino County Public Library, 300 W. Aspen Ave. (928) 779-7670

Phoenix: Phoenix Public Library, Information Services Dept., 1221 N. Central Ave. (602) 262-4636

Prescott: Prescott Public Library, 215 E. Goodwin St. (928) 777-1500

Tucson: Pima County Public Library, 101 N. Stone Ave. (520) 594-5500

Yuma: Yuma County Library District, Main Branch, 2951 S. 21st Dr. (928) 782-1871

ARKANSAS

Fayetteville: Fayetteville Public Library, 401 W. Mountain St. (479) 856-7000

Fort Smith: University of Arkansas–Fort Smith, Boreham Library, 5210 Grand Ave. (479) 788-7204

Little Rock: Central Arkansas Library System, 100 Rock St. (501) 918-3000

Little Rock: Charles A. Frueauff Foundation, 200 S. Commerce, Ste. 100 (501) 324-2233

Mountain Home: Arkansas State University, Norma Wood Library, 1600 S. College St. (870) 508-6112

CALIFORNIA

Bakersfield: Kern County Library, Beale Memorial Library, 701 Truxtun Ave. (661) 868-0701

Bayside: Rooney Resource Center, Humboldt Area Foundation, 373 Indianola Rd. (707) 442-2993

Berkeley: Berkeley Public Library, 2090 Kittredge St. (510) 981-6100

Camarillo: Ventura County Community Foundation, Center for Nonprofit Leadership, 1317 Del Norte Rd., Ste. 150 (805) 988-0196

Fairfield: Solano Community Foundation, 1261 Travis Blvd., Ste. 320 (707) 399-3846

Livermore: Las Positas College Library, 3000 Campus Hill Dr., Bldg. 2000 (925) 424-1151

Lompoc: Lompoc Public Library, 501 E. North Ave. (805) 875-8789

Long Beach: Long Beach Nonprofit Partnership, 3635 Atlantic Ave. (562) 290-0018

Los Angeles: Southern California Library for Social Studies and Research, 6120 S. Vermont Ave. (323) 759-6063

Milpitas: Compasspoint Nonprofit Services, Nonprofit Development Library, 600 Valley Way, Ste. A (408) 719-1400

Modesto: Stanislaus County Library, 1500 I St. (209) 558-7800

Monterey: Community Foundation for Monterey County, 2354 Garden Rd. (831) 375-9712

North Hills: Los Angeles Public Library, Mid-Valley Regional Branch Library, 16244 Nordhoff St. (818) 895-3654

Oakland: Oakland Public Library, 125 14th St. (510) 238-6611

Pasadena: Flintridge Foundation, 1040 Lincoln Ave., Ste. 100 (626) 449-0839

Quincy: Plumas County Library, 445 Jackson St (530) 283-6310

Redding: Shasta College, Center for Nonprofit Resources, 1504 Market St., Ste. 200 (530) 225-4385

Richmond: Richmond Public Library, 325 Civic Center Plaza (510) 620-6561

Riverside: Resource Center for Nonprofit Management, The Bobby Bonds/Cesar Chavez Community Center, 2060 University Ave., Ste. 201 (951) 686-4402

Riverside: Riverside Public Library, 3581 Mission Inn Ave. (951) 826-5201

Sacramento: Nonprofit Resource Center, 1331 Garden Highway (916) 285-1840

San Diego: Nonprofit Management Solutions, 8265 Vickers St., Ste. C (858) 292-5702

San Diego: San Diego Foundation, 2508 Historic Decatur, Ste. 200 (619) 235-2300

San Mateo: San Mateo Public Library, 55 W. 3rd Ave. (650) 522-7802

San Pedro: Los Angeles Public Library, San Pedro Regional Branch, 931 S. Gaffey St. (310) 548-7779

San Rafael: Center for Volunteer and Nonprofit Leadership of Marin, 555 Northgate Dr. (415) 479-5710

Santa Ana: Volunteer Center Orange County, 1901 E. 4th St., Ste. 100 (714) 953-5757

Santa Barbara: Santa Barbara Public Library, 40 E. Anapamu St. (805) 962-7653

Santa Monica: Santa Monica Public Library, 601 Santa Monica Blvd. (310) 458-8600

Santa Rosa: Sonoma County Library, 3rd and E Sts. (707) 545-0831

Seaside: Seaside Branch Library, 550 Harcourt Ave. (831) 899-2055

Sonora: Sierra Nonprofit Services, 591 S. Washington St. (209) 533-1093

Resources include

- America's Nonprofit Sector
- Board Member's Book
- The Foundation Center's Guide to Proposal Writing
- Foundation Directory Online Professional
- The Foundation Directory
- The Foundation Directory, Part 2
- The Foundation Directory Supplement
- Foundation Fundamentals
- Foundation Grants to Individuals
- Foundation Grants to Individuals Online
- Foundations and Public Policy
- Foundations Today Series
- The Grantseeker's Guide to Winning Proposals
- Guía para escribir propuestas
- Guide to Funding for International and Foreign Programs
- International Grantmaking IV
- National Directory of Corporate Giving
- Philanthropy Annual
- Securing Your Organization's Future
- Social Justice Grantmaking II
- The 21st Century Nonprofit: Managing in the Age of Governance

Foundation Center locations

Main

New York:
79 Fifth Ave., 2nd Fl.
(212) 620-4230

Regional Centers

Atlanta:
Hurt Bldg., 50 Hurt Plaza Ste. 150, Grand Lobby
(404) 880-0094

Cleveland:
Kent H. Smith Library
1422 Euclid Ave., Ste. 1600
(216) 861-1934

San Francisco:
312 Sutter St., Ste. 606
(415) 397-0902

Washington, DC:
1627 K St., NW, 3rd Fl.
(202) 331-1400

Soquel: Community Foundation of Santa Cruz County, 2425 Porter St., Ste. 17   (831) 477-0800

Truckee: Truckee Tahoe Community Foundation, 11071 Donner Pass Rd. (530) 587-1776

Ukiah: Catalyst (North Coast Opportunities), 776 S. State St., Ste. 102B   (707) 462-2984

Victorville: High Desert Resource Network, c/o Women's Business Center, 15490 Civic Dr., Ste. 106 (760) 949-2930

COLORADO

Colorado Springs: El Pomar Nonprofit Resource Center, Penrose Library, 20 N. Cascade Ave.   (719) 531-6333

Denver: Denver Public Library, 10 W. 14th Ave. Pkwy.   (720) 865-1111

Durango: Durango Public Library, 1900 East 3rd Ave.   (970) 375-3380

Grand Junction: Mesa County Libraries, 530 Grand Ave.   (970) 243-4443

Greeley: High Plains Library District, Farr Branch Library, 1939 61st Ave.   (970) 506-8550

Pueblo: Doris D. Kester Southern Colorado Community Foundation, Nonprofit Resource Center, Rawlings Public Library, 100 E. Abriendo Ave.   (719) 562-5626

Steamboat Springs: Yampa Valley Community Foundation, 465 Anglers Dr., Ste. 2-G (970) 879-8632

CONNECTICUT

Greenwich: Greenwich Library, 101 W. Putnam Ave.   (203) 622-7900

Hartford: Hartford Public Library, 500 Main St.   (860) 695-6295

Middletown: Russell Library, 123 Broad St.   (860) 347-2520

New Haven: New Haven Free Public Library, 133 Elm St.   (203) 946-7431

New Milford: New Milford Public Library, 24 Main St.   (860) 355-1191

Westport: Westport Public Library, Arnold Bernhard Plaza, 20 Jesup Rd. (203) 291-4800

DELAWARE

Dover: Dover Public Library, 45 S. State St.   (302) 736-7030

Newark: University of Delaware, Hugh M. Morris Library, 181 S. College Ave.   (302) 831-2432

Wilmington: University of Delaware, Center for Community Research and Service, 100 W. 10th St., Ste. 812 (302) 573-4475

FLORIDA

Bartow: Bartow Public Library, 2151 S. Broadway Ave.   (863) 534-0131

Boca Raton: Junior League of Boca Raton, Vegso Community Resource Center, 261 NW 13th St.   (561) 620-2553

Clearwater: JWB Children's Services Council of Pinellas County Grants Resource Center, 14155 58th St. N.   (727) 547-5670

Clermont: Community Foundation of South Lake County, George Hovis and Don Wickham Community and Nonprofit Resource Center, 2150 Oakley Seaver Dr. (352) 394-3818

Daytona Beach: Volusia County Library Center, City Island, 105 E. Magnolia Ave.   (386) 257-6036

Fort Lauderdale: Nova Southeastern University, Alvin Sherman Library, Research, and Information Technology Center, 3100 Ray Ferrero Jr. Blvd. (954) 262-4613

Fort Myers: Southwest Florida Community Foundation, 8260 College Pkwy., Ste. 101   (239) 274-5900

Fort Pierce: Indian River Community College, Miley Library, Learning Resources Center, 3209 Virginia Ave.   (866) 866-4722

Gainesville: Alachua County Library District, 401 E. University Ave. (352) 334-3900

Jacksonville: Jacksonville Public Libraries, 303 N. Laura St.   (904) 630-2665

Miami: Miami-Dade Public Library, Humanities/Social Science Department, 101 W. Flagler St.   (305) 375-5575

Orlando: Orange County Library System, Social Sciences Dept., 101 E. Central Blvd.   (407) 835-7323

Sarasota: Selby Public Library, 1331 1st St.   (941) 861-1100

Stuart: Martin County Library System, Blake Library, 2351 SE Monterey Rd.   (772) 288-5702

Tampa: Hillsborough County Public Library Cooperative, John F. Germany Public Library, 900 N. Ashley Dr. (813) 273-3652

West Palm Beach: Community Foundation for Palm Beach and Martin Counties, 700 S. Dixie Highway, Ste. 200 (561) 659-6800

Winter Park: Rollins College, Philanthropy and Nonprofit Leadership Center Library, 200 E. New England Ave., Ste. 250   (407) 975-6414

GEORGIA

Atlanta: Atlanta–Fulton Public Library System, Ivan Allen Jr. Reference Dept., One Margaret Mitchell Square (404) 730-1900

Brunswick: United Way of Coastal Georgia, Coastal Georgia Nonprofit Center, 1311 Union St.   (912) 265-1850

Columbus: Chattahoochee Valley Regional Library System, Columbus Public Library, 3000 Macon Rd. (706) 243-2669

Gainesville: Hall County Library System, 127 Main St. NW   (770) 532-3311

Macon: Methodist Home, Rumford Center, 304 Pierce Ave., 1st Fl.   (478) 751-2800

Savannah: Georgia Center for Nonprofits, Coastal Georgia Regional Office, 428 Bull St., Ste. 202E   (912) 234-9688

Thomasville: Thomas County Public Library, 201 N. Madison St. (229) 225-5252

Vienna: Southwest Georgia United, 1150 Industrial Dr.   (229) 268-7592

IDAHO

Boise: Boise Public Library, 715 S. Capitol Blvd.   (208) 384-4024

Coeur d'Alene: United Way of Kootenai County, 501 E. Lakeside Ave., Ste. 3   (208) 667-8112

Pocatello: Marshall Public Library, 113 S. Garfield   (208) 232-1263

ILLINOIS

Carbondale: Carbondale Public Library, 405 W. Main St.   (618) 457-0354

Chicago: Donors Forum, 208 S. LaSalle, Ste. 1535   (312) 578-0175

Evanston: Evanston Public Library, 1703 Orrington Ave.   (847) 448-8630

Glen Ellyn: College of DuPage, Philanthropy Center, Student Resource Center, 425 Fawell Blvd. (630) 942-3364

Grayslake: College of Lake County, John C. Murphy Memorial Library, Lake County Philanthropy Center, 19351 W. Washington St. (847) 543-2071

Oak Forest: Acorn Public Library, 15624 S. Central Ave.   (708) 687-3700

Quincy: John Wood Community College, West Central Illinois Philanthropy Center, 1301 S. 48th St. (217) 224-6500

Rock Island: Rock Island Public Library, 401 19th St.   (309) 732-7323

Schaumburg: Schaumburg Township District Library, Northwest Suburban Philanthropy Center, 130 S. Roselle Rd.   (847) 985-4000

Springfield: University of Illinois at Springfield, Central Illinois Nonprofit Resources Center, Brookens Library, One University Plaza, MS BRK 140   (217) 206-6633

INDIANA

Anderson: Anderson Public Library, 111 E. 12th St.   (765) 641-2456

Bloomington: Monroe County Public Library, 303 E. Kirkwood Ave. (812) 349-3050

Evansville: Evansville Vanderburgh Public Library, 200 SE Martin Luther King Jr. Blvd.   (812) 428-8218

Fort Wayne: Allen County Public Library, Paul Clarke Nonprofit Resource Center, 900 Library Plaza   (260) 421-1238

Gary: Indiana University Northwest, 3400 Broadway   (219) 980-6580

Indianapolis: First Samuel (W) Holistic Resource Center, 1402 N. Belleview Place (317) 636-7653

Indianapolis: Indianapolis–Marion County Public Library, 40 E. St. Clair St. (317) 275-4100

Muncie: Muncie Public Library, 2005 S. High St.   (765) 747-8204

Shelbyville: Shelbyville–Shelby County Public Library, 57 W. Broadway St.   (317) 398-7121

Terre Haute: Vigo County Public Library, One Library Square   (812) 232-1113

Valparaiso: Valparaiso University, Christopher Center for Library and Information Resources, 1410 Chapel Dr.   (219) 464-5364

Washington: Carnegie Public Library, 300 W. Main St.   (812) 254-4586

IOWA

Ames: Iowa State University, 204 Parks Library   (515) 294-3642

Cedar Rapids: Cedar Rapids Public Library, 2600 Edgewood Rd. SW (319) 398-5123

Council Bluffs: Council Bluffs Public Library, 400 Willow Ave. (712) 323-7553

Des Moines: Des Moines Public Library, 1000 Grand Ave.   (515) 283-4152

Dubuque: Community Foundation of Greater Dubuque, 700 Locust St., Ste. 195   (563) 588-2700

Fairfield: Fairfield Public Library, 104 W. Adams   (641) 472-6551

Sioux City: Sioux City Public Library, Siouxland Funding Research Center, 529 Pierce St.   (712) 255-2933

KANSAS

Colby: Pioneer Memorial Library, 375 W. 4th St.   (785) 460-4470

Ellis: Ellis Public Library, 907 Washington St.   (785) 726-3464

Junction City: Dorothy Bramlage Public Library, 230 W. 7th St.   (785) 238-4311

Liberal: Liberal Memorial Library, 519 N. Kansas   (620) 626-0180

Ness City: Ness City Public Library, 113 S. Iowa Ave.   (785) 798-3415

Salina: Salina Public Library, 301 W. Elm   (785) 825-4624

Topeka: Topeka and Shawnee County Public Library, Adult Services, 1515 SW 10th Ave.   (785) 580-4400

Wichita: Wichita Public Library, 223 S. Main St.   (316) 261-8500

KENTUCKY

Bowling Green: Western Kentucky University, Helm–Cravens Library, 110 Helm Library   (270) 745-6163

Covington: Kenton County Public Library, 502 Scott Blvd.   (859) 962-4060

Lexington: Lexington Public Library, 140 E. Main St.   (859) 231-5520

Louisville: Bellarmine University, W.L. Lyons Brown Library, 2001 Newburg Rd.   (502) 452-8317

Louisville: Louisville Free Public Library, 301 York St.   (502) 574-1617

Somerset: Pulaski County Public Library, 304 S. Main St.   (606) 679-8401

LOUISIANA

Alexandria: Community Development Works, 1101 4th St., Ste. 101B (318) 443-7880

Baton Rouge: East Baton Rouge Parish Library, River Center Branch, 120 St. Louis St.   (225) 389-4967

Baton Rouge: Louisiana Association of Nonprofit Organizations (LANO), 4560 North Blvd., Ste. 117 (225) 343-5266

DeRidder: Beauregard Parish Library, 205 S. Washington Ave. (337) 463-6217

Lafayette: Louisiana Association of Nonprofit Organizations (LANO), Community Foundation of Acadiana, 600 Jefferson St., Ste. 402 (337) 266-2145

New Orleans: Louisiana Association of Nonprofit Organizations (LANO), 1824 Oretha Castle Haley Blvd. (504) 309-2081

New Orleans: New Orleans Public Library, Business and Science Division, 219 Loyola Ave.   (504) 596-2580

Shreveport: Louisiana Association of Nonprofit Organizations (LANO), 2924 Knight St., Ste. 406 (318) 865-5510

Shreveport: Shreve Memorial Library, 424 Texas St.   (318) 226-5894

MAINE

Portland: Maine Philanthropy Center, USM Glickman Family Library, 314 Forest Ave., Room 321 (207) 780-5039

MARYLAND

Baltimore: Enoch Pratt Free Library, Social Science and History Dept., 400 Cathedral St. (410) 396-5320

Columbia: Howard County Library, Central Library, 10375 Little Patuxent Pkwy. (410) 313-7860

Frederick: Frederick County Public Libraries, C. Burr Artz Central Library, 110 E. Patrick St. (301) 600-1383

Hagerstown: Washington County Free Library, 100 S. Potomac St. (301) 739-3250

Hyattsville: Prince George's County Memorial Library, Hyattsville Branch Library, 6530 Adelphi Rd. (301) 985-4690

Prince Frederick: Calvert Library, 850 Costley Way (410) 535-0291

Rockville: Rockville Library, 21 Maryland Ave. (240) 777-0140

Salisbury: Community Foundation of the Eastern Shore, 1324 Belmont Ave. (410) 724-9911

Waldorf: Charles County Public Library, P.D. Brown Memorial Branch, 50 Village St. (301) 645-2864

Wye Mills: Chesapeake College Library, 1000 College Dr. (410) 827-5860

MASSACHUSETTS

Boston: Associated Grant Makers (AGM), 55 Court St., Ste. 520 (617) 426-2606

Boston: Boston Public Library, Social Sciences Reference Dept., 700 Boylston St. (617) 536-5400

Oak Bluffs: Oak Bluffs Public Library, 56R School St. (508) 693-9433

Pittsfield: Berkshire Athenaeum, One Wendell Ave. (413) 499-9480

Springfield: Springfield City Library, 220 State St. (413) 263-6828

West Barnstable: Cape Cod Community College, Wilkens Library, 2240 Iyannough Rd. (508) 362-2131 x4480

Worcester: Worcester Public Library, 3 Salem Square (508) 799-1654

MEXICO

Guanajuato: Biblioteca Publica de San Miguel de Allende, A.C., Insurgentes 25, San Miguel de Allende (+52) 415-152-0293

Querétaro, Qro: International Resource Center for Civil Society Organizations in Mexico, Av. Senda Eterna #461, Tower Robles-1, Milenio III (+52) 442-229-1537

MICHIGAN

Alpena: Alpena County Library, 211 N. 1st St. (989) 356-6188

Ann Arbor: University of Michigan, Harlan Hatcher Graduate Library, 209 Hatcher Graduate Library (734) 615-8610

Battle Creek: Willard Public Library, 7 W. Van Buren St. (269) 968-3284

Detroit: Purdy/Kresge Library, Wayne State University, 134 Purdy/Kresge Library (313) 577-6424

East Lansing: Michigan State University, Funding Center, 100 Library (517) 432-6123

Farmington Hills: Farmington Community Library, 32737 W. 12 Mile Rd. (248) 553-0300

Flint: Flint Public Library, 1026 E. Kearsley St. (810) 232-7111

Fremont: Fremont Area District Library, 104 E. Main St. (231) 924-3480

Grand Rapids: Grand Rapids Public Library, Reference Dept., 111 Library St. NE (616) 988-5400

Houghton: Portage Lake District Library, 58 Huron St. (906) 482-4570

Kalamazoo: Kalamazoo Public Library, 315 S. Rose St. (269) 553-7844

Ludington: Mason County District Library, Ludington Library, 217 E. Ludington Ave. (231) 843-8465

Marquette: Peter White Public Library, 217 N. Front St. (906) 226-4311

Petoskey: Petoskey Public Library, 500 E. Mitchell St. (231) 758-3100

Saginaw: Public Libraries of Saginaw, Hoyt Public Library, 505 Janes Ave. (989) 755-0904

Traverse City: Traverse Area District Library, 610 Woodmere Ave. (231) 932-8500

Washington: Romeo District Library, Graubner Library, 65821 Van Dyke (586) 752-0603

MINNESOTA

Brainerd: Brainerd Public Library, 416 S. 5th St. (218) 829-5574

Duluth: Duluth Public Library, 520 W. Superior St. (218) 730-4200

Mankato: Blue Earth County Library, 100 E. Main St. (507) 304-4001

Marshall: Southwest Minnesota State University, University Library, 1501 State St. (507) 537-7278

Minneapolis: Hennepin County Library, Minneapolis Central Library, 300 Nicollet Mall (612) 630-6000

Rochester: Rochester Public Library, 101 2nd St. SE (507) 328-2300

St. Cloud: Central Minnesota Community Foundation, 101 S. 7th Ave., Ste. 100 (320) 253-4380

St. Paul: St. Paul Public Library, 90 W. 4th St. (651) 266-7000

MISSISSIPPI

Hattiesburg: Library of Hattiesburg, Petal and Forrest County, 329 Hardy St. (601) 582-4461

Jackson: Jackson/Hinds Library System, 300 N. State St. (601) 968-5803

MISSOURI

Columbia: Columbia/Boone County Community Partnership, 1900 N. Providence, Ste. 300 (573) 256-1890

Kansas City: Kansas City Public Library, 14 W. 10th St. (816) 701-3400

Kirkwood: Kirkwood Public Library, 200 S. Kirkwood Rd. (314) 821-5770

Springfield: Springfield-Greene County Library, 4653 S. Campbell (417) 882-0714

St. Louis: St. Louis Public Library, 1301 Olive St. (314) 241-2288

St. Peters: St. Charles City-County Library District, Spencer Road Branch, 427 Spencer Rd. (636) 441-0794

MONTANA

Baker: Fallon County Library, 6 W. Fallon Ave. (406) 778-7160

Billings: Montana State University–Billings, Library–Special Collections, 1500 University Dr. (406) 657-2262

Bozeman: Bozeman Public Library, 626 E. Main St. (406) 582-2402

Kalispell: Flathead County Library, 247 1st Ave. E. (406) 758-5819

Missoula: University of Montana, Mansfield Library, 32 Campus Dr. #9936 (406) 243-6800

NEBRASKA

Cambridge: Butler Memorial Library, 621 Penn St. (308) 697-3836

Hastings: Hastings Public Library, 517 W. 4th St. (402) 461-2346

Lincoln: University of Nebraska–Lincoln, Love Library, 13th and R Sts. (402) 472-2526

Omaha: Omaha Public Library, W. Dale Clark (Main) Library, 215 S. 15th St. (402) 444-4826

NEVADA

Carson City: Nevada State Library and Archives, 100 N. Stewart St. (775) 684-3314

Elko: Great Basin College Library, 1500 College Pkwy. (775) 753-2222

Incline Village: Parasol Community Collaboration, 948 Incline Way (775) 298-0118

Las Vegas: Clark County Library, 1401 E. Flamingo 702-507-3421

NEW HAMPSHIRE

Concord: Concord Public Library, 45 Green St. (603) 225-8670

Plymouth: Plymouth State University, Herbert H. Lamson Library, 17 High St. (603) 535-2258

NEW JERSEY

Elizabeth: Free Public Library of Elizabeth, 11 S. Broad St. (908) 354-6060

Galloway: United Way of Atlantic County, 4 E. Jimmie Leeds Rd., Ste. 10 (609) 404-4483

Piscataway: Piscataway Public Library, John F. Kennedy Branch, 500 Hoes Lane (732) 463-1633

Randolph: County College of Morris, Learning Resource Center, 214 Center Grove Rd. (973) 328-5296

Trenton: New Jersey State Library, 185 W. State St. (609) 278-2640

Vineland: Cumberland County College, Center for Leadership, Community and Neighborhood Development, 3322 College Dr. (856) 691-8600

Washington: Warren County Community College, 475 Rte. 57 W. (908) 835-9222

NEW MEXICO

Albuquerque: Albuquerque/Bernalillo County Library System, 501 Copper Ave. NW (505) 768-5141

Las Cruces: Thomas Branigan Memorial Library, 200 E. Picacho Ave. (575) 528-4000

Santa Fe: New Mexico State Library, 1209 Camino Carlos Rey (505) 476-9702

NEW YORK

Albany: New York State Library, Cultural Education Center, Empire State Plaza (518) 474-5355

Auburn: Seymour Public Library District, 176-178 Genesee St. (315) 252-2571

Binghamton: Broome County Public Library, 185 Court St. (607) 778-6400

Bronx: New York Public Library, Bronx Library Center, 310 E. Kingsbridge Rd. (718) 579-4244

Brooklyn: Brooklyn Public Library, Society, Sciences, and Technology Division, 10 Grand Army Plaza (718) 230-2145

Buffalo: Buffalo and Erie County Public Library, Business, Science, and Technology Dept., One Lafayette Square (716) 858-8900

Cobleskill: SUNY Cobleskill, Jared Van Wagenen Library, 142 Schenectady Ave. (518) 255-5841

Corning: Southeast Steuben County Library, 300 Nasser Civic Center Plaza (607) 936-3713

Flushing: Queens Borough Public Library, Flushing Branch, 41-17 Main St. (718) 661-1200

Holbrook: Sachem Public Library, 150 Holbrook Rd. (631) 588-5024

Huntington: Huntington Public Library, 338 Main St. (631) 427-5165

Jamaica: Queens Borough Public Library, Social Sciences Division, 89-11 Merrick Blvd. (718) 990-0700

Jamestown: James Prendergast Library, 509 Cherry St. (716) 484-7135

Kingston: Kingston Library, 55 Franklin St. (845) 331-0507

Levittown: Levittown Public Library, One Bluegrass Lane (516) 731-5728

Mahopac: Mahopac Public Library, 668 Rte. 6 (845) 628-2009

Margaretville: Blue Deer Center, 1155 County Rte. 6 (845) 586-3225

New York: New York Public Library, Countee Cullen Branch, 104 W. 136th St. (212) 491-2070

Newburgh: Newburgh Free Library, 124 Grand St. (845) 563-3601

Poughkeepsie: Adriance Memorial Library, 18 Bancroft Rd. (845) 485-3445

Riverhead: Riverhead Free Library, 330 Court St. (631) 727-3228

Rochester: Rochester Public Library, 115 South Ave. (585) 428-8127

Saratoga Springs: Saratoga Springs Public Library, 49 Henry St. (518) 584-7860

Staten Island: New York Public Library, St. George Library Center, 5 Central Ave. (718) 442-8560

Staten Island: Wagner College, Horrmann Library, One Campus Rd. (718) 390-3401

Suffern: Suffern Free Library, 210 Lafayette Ave. (845) 357-1237

Syracuse: Onondaga County Public Library, 447 S. Salina St. (315) 435-1900

Utica: Utica Public Library, 303 Genesee St. (315) 735-2279

White Plains: White Plains Public Library, 100 Martine Ave. (914) 422-1480

Yonkers: Yonkers Public Library, Riverfront Library, One Larkin Center (914) 337-1500

NIGERIA

Maryland, Lagos: Development Alternatives and Resource Center (DARC), 2A, Akin Ademokoya Close, Off Okupe Estate Rd. (+234) 1-851-2678

NORTH CAROLINA

Asheville: Pack Memorial Library, Community Foundation of Western North Carolina, 67 Haywood St. (828) 250-4711

Brevard: Transylvania County Library, 212 S. Gaston St. (828) 884-3151

Charlotte: Public Library of Charlotte and Mecklenburg County, 310 N. Tryon St. (704) 416-0101

Durham: Durham County Public Library, 300 N. Roxboro St. (919) 560-0100

Greensboro: Greensboro Public Library, Glenwood Branch Nonprofit Resource Center, 1901 W. Florida St. (336) 297-5000

Jacksonville: Onslow County Public Library, 58 Doris Ave. E. (910) 455-7350

Kinston: Neuse Regional Library, Kinston–Lenoir County Public Library, 510 N. Queen St. (252) 527-7066

Raleigh: Wake County Public Libraries, Cameron Village Library, 1930 Clark Ave. (919) 856-6710

Spruce Pine: Avery-Mitchell-Yancey (AMY) Regional Library, Spruce Pine Public Library, 142 Walnut Ave. (828) 765-4673

Wilmington: New Hanover County Public Library, 201 Chestnut St. (910) 798-6301

Winston-Salem: Forsyth County Public Library, 660 W. 5th St. (336) 703-3020

NORTH DAKOTA

Bismarck: Bismarck Public Library, 515 N. 5th St. (701) 222-6410

Fargo: Fargo Public Library, 102 N. 3rd St. (701) 241-1472

Minot: Minot Public Library, 516 2nd Ave. SW (701) 852-1045

OHIO

Akron: Akron-Summit County Public Library, 60 S. High St. (330) 643-9000

Akron: Center for Nonprofit Excellence, 703 S. Main St., Ste. 200 (330) 762-9670

Ashtabula: Ashtabula County District Library, 335 W. 44th St. (440) 997-9341

Canton: Stark County District Library, 715 Market Ave. N. (330) 452-0665

Cincinnati: Public Library of Cincinnati and Hamilton County, 800 Vine St. (513) 369-6900

Cleveland Heights: Cleveland Heights-University Heights Public Library, Lee Road Library Branch, 2345 Lee Rd. (216) 932-3600

Columbus: Columbus Metropolitan Library, Business and Technology Dept., 96 S. Grant Ave. (614) 645-2275

Dayton: Dayton Metro Library, 215 E. 3rd St. (937) 463-2665

Elyria: Elyria Public Library, West River Branch, 1194 W. River Road N. (440) 324-9827

Independence: Cuyahoga County Public Library, Independence Branch, 6361 Selig Dr. (216) 447-4926

Lima: Lima Public Library, 650 W. Market St. (419) 228-5113

Mansfield: Mansfield/Richland County Public Library, 43 W. 3rd St. (419) 521-3110

Marietta: Marietta College, Legacy Library, 220 5th St. (740) 376-4741

Painesville: Morley Library, 184 Phelps St. (440) 352-3383

Piqua: Edison Community College Library, 1973 Edison Dr. (937) 778-7950

Portsmouth: Portsmouth Public Library, 1220 Gallia St. (740) 354-5688

Toledo: Toledo-Lucas County Public Library, Business Technology Dept., 325 N. Michigan St. (419) 259-5209

Twinsburg: Twinsburg Public Library, 10050 Ravenna Rd. (330) 425-4268

Warren: Kent State University, Trumbull Campus Library, 4314 Mahoning Ave. NW (330) 847-0571

Westlake: Westlake Porter Public Library, 27333 Center Ridge Rd. (440) 871-2600

Wooster: Wayne County Public Library, 220 W. Liberty St. (330) 262-0916

Youngstown: Public Library of Youngstown and Mahoning County, 305 Wick Ave. (330) 744-8636

Zanesville: Muskingum County Community Foundation, 534 Putnam Ave. (740) 453-5192

OKLAHOMA

Durant: Southeastern Oklahoma State University, Henry G. Bennett Memorial Library, 1405 N. 4th, PMB 4105 (580) 745-2702

Enid: Public Library of Enid and Garfield County, 120 W. Maine (580) 234-6313

Oklahoma City: Oklahoma City University, Dulaney Browne Library, 2501 N. Blackwelder (405) 208-5065

Tulsa: Tulsa City–County Library, 400 Civic Center (918) 596-7977

OREGON

Eugene: University of Oregon, Knight Library, 1501 Kincaid (541) 346-3053

Klamath Falls: Oregon Institute of Technology Library, 3201 Campus Dr. (541) 885-1000

Medford: Jackson County Library Services, 205 S. Central Ave. (541) 774-8689

Portland: Multnomah County Library, Government Documents, 801 SW 10th Ave. (503) 988-5123

PENNSYLVANIA

Aliquippa: Beaver County Library System, 109 Pleasant Dr., Ste. 101 (724) 728-3737

Allentown: Allentown Public Library, 1210 Hamilton St. (610) 820-2400

Bethlehem: Northampton Community College, Paul and Harriett Mack Library, 3835 Green Pond Rd. (610) 861-5360

Blue Bell: Montgomery County Community College, The Brendlinger Library, 340 DeKalb Pike (215) 641-6596

Bristol: Margaret R. Grundy Memorial Library, 680 Radcliffe St. (215) 788-7891

Erie: Erie County Library System, 160 E. Front St. (814) 451-6927

Franklin: Franklin Public Library, 421 12th St. (814) 432-5062

Harrisburg: Dauphin County Library System, East Shore Area Library, 4501 Ethel St. (717) 652-9380

Hazleton: Hazleton Area Public Library, 55 N. Church St. (570) 454-2961

Honesdale: Wayne County Public Library, 1406 N. Main St. (570) 253-1220

Lancaster: Lancaster Public Library, 125 N. Duke St. (717) 394-2651

Philadelphia: Free Library of Philadelphia, Regional Foundation Center, 1901 Vine St., 2nd Fl. (215) 686-5423

Philadelphia: The Johnson-UGO Foundation Library, Johnson Memorial UMC Education Building, 3117 Longshore Ave. (215) 338-5020

Phoenixville: Phoenixville Public Library, 183 2nd Ave. (610) 933-3013

Pittsburgh: Carnegie Library of Pittsburgh, 612 Smithfield St. (412) 281-7143

Pittston: Nonprofit and Community Assistance Center, 1151 Oak St. (570) 655-5581

Reading: Reading Public Library, 100 S. 5th St. (610) 655-6355

Scranton: Albright Memorial Library, 500 Vine St. (570) 348-3000

Sharon: Community Library of the Shenango Valley, 11 N. Sharpsville Ave. (724) 981-4360

Williamsport: James V. Brown Library, 19 E. 4th St. (570) 326-0536

York: Martin Library, 159 E. Market St. (717) 846-5300

PUERTO RICO

San Juan: Universidad Del Sagrado Corazón, Biblioteca Madre Maria Teresa Guevara, PO Box 12383 (787) 728-1515

RHODE ISLAND

Providence: Providence Public Library, 150 Empire St. (401) 455-8088

SOUTH CAROLINA

Anderson: Anderson County Library, 300 N. McDuffie St. (864) 260-4500

Charleston: Charleston County Library, 68 Calhoun St. (843) 805-6930

Columbia: South Carolina State Library, 1500 Senate St. (803) 734-8026

Florence: Florence County Library System, Doctors Bruce and Lee Foundation Headquarters Library, 509 S. Dargan St. (843) 662-8424

Greenville: Greenville County Library System, 25 Heritage Green Place (864) 242-5000

Spartanburg: Spartanburg County Public Libraries, 151 S. Church St. (864) 596-3500

SOUTH DAKOTA

Madison: Dakota State University, 820 N. Washington (605) 256-5100

Pierre: South Dakota State Library, 800 Governors Dr. (605) 773-3131

Rapid City: Rapid City Public Library, 610 Quincy St. (605) 394-4171

SOUTH KOREA

Seoul: The Beautiful Foundation, 16-3 Gahoe-dong, Jongno-Gu (+82) 2-766-1004

TENNESSEE

Chattanooga: United Way of Greater Chattanooga, 630 Market St. (423) 752-0300

Johnson City: Johnson City Public Library, 100 W. Millard St. (423) 434-4450

Knoxville: Knox County Public Library, 500 W. Church Ave. (865) 215-8751

Memphis: Alliance for Nonprofit Excellence, 606 S. Mendenhall, Ste. 108 (901) 684-6605

Memphis: Memphis Public Library and Information Center, 3030 Poplar Ave. (901) 415-2734

Nashville: Nashville Public Library, 615 Church St. (615) 862-5800

TEXAS

Amarillo: Amarillo Area Foundation, 801 S. Filmore, Ste. 700 (806) 376-4521

Arlington: Arlington Public Library, George W. Hawkes Central Library, 101 E. Abram St. (817) 459-6900

Austin: Regional Foundation Library, 1009 East 11th St. (512) 475-7373

Beaumont: Southeast Texas Nonprofit Development Center, 700 North St., Suite D (409) 832-6565

Corpus Christi: Corpus Christi Public Library, 805 Comanche St. (361) 880-7000

Dallas: Dallas Public Library, Urban Information, 1515 Young St. (214) 670-1400

Edinburg: Southwest Border Nonprofit Resource Center, The University of Texas-Pan American, 1201 West University Drive, ITT 1.404H (956) 292-7566

El Paso: University of Texas at El Paso, Community Non-Profit Grant Library, 500 W. University, Benedict Hall Room 103 (915) 747-5672

Fort Worth: Funding Information Center of Fort Worth, 329 S. Henderson St. (817) 334-0228

Houston: Houston Public Library, Bibliographic Information Center, 500 McKinney St. (832) 393-1313

Houston: United Way of Greater Houston, 50 Waugh Dr. (713) 685-2300

Kingsville: Texas A&M University–Kingsville, James C. Jernigan Library, 700 University Blvd., MSC 197 (361) 593-3416

Laredo: Nonprofit Management and Volunteer Center, 1301 Farragut St., Transit Center, 2nd Fl., East Wing (956) 795-2675

Longview: Longview Public Library, 222 W. Cotton St. (903) 237-1350

Lubbock: Lubbock Area Foundation, 1655 Main St., Ste. 209 (806) 762-8061

North Richland Hills: North Richland Hills Public Library, 9015 Grand Ave. (817) 427-6800

San Antonio: Nonprofit Resource Center of Texas, 110 Broadway, Ste. 230 (210) 227-4333

Tyler: United Way of Tyler/Smith County, 4000 Southpark Dr. (903) 581-6376

Waco: Waco-McLennan County Library, 1717 Austin Ave. (254) 750-5941

Wichita Falls: Nonprofit Management Center of Wichita Falls, 2301 Kell Blvd., Ste. 218 (940) 322-4961

THAILAND

Chiang Mai: Payap University–Funding Resource Center, Sirindhorn Learning Resource Center (Central Library), Super-highway Chiang Mai–Lumpang Rd., Amphur Muang (+66) 53-851-478 x7450

UTAH

Cedar City: Southern Utah University, Gerald R. Sherratt Library, 351 W. University Blvd. (435) 586-7700

Moab: Grand County Public Library, 257 E. Center St. (435) 259-5421

Ogden: United Way of Northern Utah, Zada Haws Community Grant Center, 2955 Harrison Blvd., Ste. 201 (801) 399-5584

Salt Lake City: Salt Lake City Public Library, 210 E. 400 S. (801) 524-8200

Salt Lake City: Utah Nonprofits Association, 175 S. Main St., Ste. 1210 (801) 596-1800

VERMONT

Middlebury: Ilsley Public Library, 75 Main St. (802) 388-4095

Montpelier: Vermont Dept. of Libraries, Reference and Law Information Services, 109 State St. (802) 828-3261

VIRGINIA

Abingdon: Washington County Public Library, 205 Oak Hill St. (276) 676-6222

Alexandria: Alexandria Library, Kate Waller Barrett Branch, 717 Queen St. (703) 838-4555

Arlington: Arlington County Public Library, 1015 N. Quincy St. (703) 228-5990

Ashburn: George Washington University, Virginia Campus Library, 44983 Knoll Square, Ste. 179 (703) 726-8230

Bealeton: Fauquier County Public Library, Bealeton Library, 10877 Willow Dr. N. (540) 439-9728

Charlottesville: Center for Nonprofit Excellence, 401 E. Market St., Exec. Ste. 26 and 27 (434) 244-3330

Fairfax: Fairfax County Public Library, 12000 Government Center Pkwy., Ste. 329 (703) 324-3100

Fredericksburg: Central Rappahannock Regional Library, 1201 Caroline St. (540) 372-1144

Hampton: Hampton Public Library, 4207 Victoria Blvd. (757) 727-1314

Hopewell: Appomattox Regional Library System, 209 E. Cawson St. (804) 458-0110

Norfolk: VOLUNTEER Hampton Roads, 400 W. Olney Rd., Ste. B (757) 624-2400

Richmond: Richmond Public Library, Business, Science and Technology, 101 E. Franklin St. (804) 646-7223

Roanoke: Roanoke City Public Library System, 706 S. Jefferson St. (540) 853-2477

Sperryville: Rappahannock NonProfit Center, 12018 A Lee Highway (540) 987-8011

Virginia Beach: Virginia Beach Public Library, 4100 Virginia Beach Blvd. (757) 385-0120

WASHINGTON

Bellingham: Bellingham Public Library, 210 Central Ave. (360) 778-7323

Bremerton: United Way of Kitsap County, 746 4th St. (360) 377-8505

Kennewick: Mid-Columbia Library, 1620 S. Union St. (509) 783-7878

Redmond: King County Library System, Redmond Regional Library, Nonprofit and Philanthropy Resource Center, 15990 NE 85th (425) 885-1861

Seattle: Seattle Public Library, 1000 4th Ave. (206) 386-4636

Spokane: Spokane Public Library, 906 W. Main Ave. (509) 444-5300

Tacoma: University of Washington Tacoma Library, 1902 Commerce St. (253) 692-4440

WEST VIRGINIA

Bluefield: Craft Memorial Library, 600 Commerce St. (304) 325-3943

Charleston: Kanawha County Public Library, 123 Capitol St. (304) 343-4646

Parkersburg: West Virginia University at Parkersburg, 300 Campus Dr. (304) 424-8260

Shepherdstown: Shepherd University, Ruth A. Scarborough Library, 301 N. King St. (304) 876-5420

Wheeling: Wheeling Jesuit University, Bishop Hodges Library, 316 Washington Ave. (304) 243-2226

WISCONSIN

Eau Claire: L.E. Phillips Memorial Public Library, 400 Eau Claire St. (715) 839-5001

Madison: University of Wisconsin—Madison, Memorial Library, Grants Information Center, 728 State St., Room 262 (608) 262-3242

Milwaukee: Marquette University Raynor Memorial Library, 1355 W. Wisconsin Ave. (414) 288-1515

Stevens Point: University of Wisconsin–Stevens Point, 900 Reserve St. (715) 346-2540

WYOMING

Casper: Natrona County Public Library, 307 E. 2nd St. (307) 237-4935

Cheyenne: Laramie County Community College, Ludden Library, 1400 E. College Dr. (307) 778-1205

Gillette: Campbell County Public Library, 2101 S. 4-J Rd. (307) 687-0115

Jackson: Teton County Library, 125 Virginian Lane (307) 733-2164

Sheridan: Sheridan County Fulmer Public Library, 335 W. Alger St. (307) 674-8585

FOUNDATION CENTER
Knowledge to build on.

About the Foundation Center Established in 1956 and today supported by close to 600 foundations, the Foundation Center is the nation's leading authority on philanthropy, connecting nonprofits and the grantmakers supporting them to tools they can use and information they can trust. The Center maintains the most comprehensive database on U.S. grantmakers and their grants—a robust, accessible knowledge bank for the sector. It also operates research, education, and training programs designed to advance knowledge of philanthropy at every level. Thousands of people visit the Center's web site each day and are served in its five regional library/learning centers and its network of more than 400 funding information centers located in public libraries, community foundations, and educational institutions in every U.S. state and beyond. For more information, please visit foundationcenter.org or call (212) 620-4230.

Interested in Becoming a Cooperating Collection? Cooperating Collections provide underresourced and underserved populations across the U.S. with crucial information and education. To expand the network in regions where nonprofit communities are most in need of Foundation Center resources, we welcome proposals from qualified institutions—public, academic, or special libraries; community foundations; nonprofit resource centers; and other technical assistance providers—that can partner with us to help grantseekers succeed. If you are interested in establishing a Collection in your area or would like to learn more about the program, please visit foundationcenter.org/collections or contact: Coordinator of Cooperating Collections, Foundation Center, 79 Fifth Avenue, New York, NY 10003. E-mail: ccmail@foundationcenter.org